A complete spelling programme
Year 2

raintree
a Capstone company — publishers for children

Babcock ldp
partners in education

Raintree is an imprint of Capstone Global Library Limited, a company incorporated in
England and Wales having its registered office at 7 Pilgrim Street, London, EC4V 6LB –
Registered company number: 6695582

www.raintree.co.uk
myorders@raintree.co.uk

Text © Capstone Global Library Limited 2016
The moral rights of the proprietor have been asserted.

Devised and written by Rebecca Cosgrave, Jenny Core, Joy Simpson and Angela Sykes
        of the Babcock LDP Primary English Team.
Edited by Clare Lewis
Designed by Richard Parker and HL Studios
Picture research by Eric Gohl
Production by Helen McCreath
Originated by Capstone Global Library Ltd
Printed at Ashford Colour Press, Gosport, Hants

ISBN 978 1 4747 0998 9
19 18 17 16 15
10 9 8 7 6 5 4 3 2 1

Pack
ISBN 978 1 4747 0981 1
19 18 17 16 15
10 9 8 7 6 5 4 3 2 1

British Library Cataloguing in Publication Data
A full catalogue record for this book is available from the British Library.

Acknowledgements
National Curriculum extract p. 11 © Crown copyright information licensed under the
Open Government Licence v3.0.

All photographs provided by Shutterstock

Every effort has been made to contact copyright holders of material reproduced
in this book. Any omissions will be rectified in subsequent printings if notice is given
to the publisher.

All the Internet addresses (URLs) given in this book were valid at the time of going to
press. However, due to the dynamic nature of the Internet, some addresses may have
changed, or sites may have changed or ceased to exist since publication. While the
author and publisher regret any inconvenience this may cause readers, no responsibility
for any such changes can be accepted by either the author or the publisher.

Contents

Introduction

What is the *No Nonsense Spelling* Programme?

The *No Nonsense Spelling* Programme was devised to offer teachers a comprehensive yet accessible progression in the teaching of spelling. Guidance, rather than prescription, is provided on how to teach the strategies, knowledge and skills pupils need to learn.

The focus of the programme is on the *teaching* of spelling, which embraces knowledge of spelling conventions – patterns and rules; but integral to the teaching is the opportunity to promote the *learning* of spellings, including statutory words, common exceptions and personal spellings.

The programme

- delivers a manageable tool for meeting the requirements of the 2014 National Curriculum
- has a clear progression through blocks of teaching units across the year
- comprehensively explains how to teach spelling effectively.

How *No Nonsense Spelling* is organised

The programme consists of the following elements:

- The requirements of the National Curriculum, which have been organised into strands and then broken down into termly overviews. The overall pathway can be found on the USB stick.
- Termly overviews that have been mapped across weeks as half termly plans. These follow a model of five spelling sessions across two weeks, except in Year 2 where sessions are daily.
- Daily lesson plans for each session, with Supporting Resources, including word lists and guidance on conventions.

The lesson plans

The lessons themselves then follow the structure below:

Lesson	*Reference to year group, block of lessons and lesson number in sequence*
Lesson type	*Revise/Teach/Learn/Practise/Apply/Assess*
Lesson focus	*The particular spelling focus for the day*
Resources needed	*A list of the resources that will be needed. These might be documents that are photocopied or printed in advance so that flashcards can be prepared, or presentations to display the task/activity on a whiteboard. The resources are featured at the end of each book for reference. Editable versions are available on the USB stick, which can be copied and pasted into your own documents and edited.*
Teaching activity	*Key teaching points, sometimes including extra notes and tips for the teacher*

Each lesson is approximately 10 to15 minutes long, but lesson plans are flexible so that the teaching can reflect the extra time needed on a teaching point if required. The Supporting Resources at the back of each book can be used as appropriate to adjust the pace and focus of the lesson. Each lesson clearly signposts when additional resources from the Programme can be used.

Supporting Resources

The Supporting Resources include pictures and word lists, which can be photocopied and made into flashcards or used in classroom displays, and pictures. They also include games and quizzes. The Resources are featured at the end of each book for reference and as editable Word documents on the USB stick, which can be copied and pasted to be used on classroom whiteboards and in other documents.

Teaching sequence

The programme has been written broadly following a teaching sequence for spelling, whereby each new concept is taught, practised and then applied and assessed. Frequently there is also a 'Revise' session before the teaching session. A typical teaching sequence is as follows:

Revise
Activate prior knowledge
Revisit previous linked learning
↓
Teach
Introduce the new concept
Explain
Investigate
Model
↓
Practise
Individual/group work
Extend/explore the concept independently
Investigate
Generalise
↓
Apply/Assess
Assess through independent application
Explain and demonstrate understanding

Within the lessons, the particular focus is identified, followed by suggested teaching strategies.

By integrating activities for handwriting, the benefit of making a spelling activity kinaesthetic is secured. The pupil acquires the physical memory of the spelling pattern as well as the visual. Integral to the process is the scope to encourage pupils to learn spellings. The value of a school policy and possible approaches are explored further on page 9, 'Learning spellings'.

You will find the following referred to in the lessons:
Modelling: An activity is described, and it is anticipated that the action expected of pupils is modelled to them first.
Spelling partners: Pupils are asked to work in pairs, often to 'test' each other. They will be asked to work with their spelling partner from time to time.

Assessment

Pupils' learning is assessed throughout the programme. The 'Apply' part of the sequence regularly includes assessment activities to identify if pupils have learnt the key concept taught. These activities include:

- Testing – by teacher and peers
- Dictation
- Explaining
- Independent application in writing
- Frequent learning and testing of statutory and personal words.

Error Analysis

Error Analysis can be used to assess what strategies pupils are using in their day-to-day writing. It can also help identify where to put emphasis in the programme – for the whole class, groups or individuals. Error Analysis can also be repeated to assess progress over a longer period of time.

A template for a suggested grid for Error Analysis can be found in the Supporting Resources.

How to complete an Error Analysis:

1 Choose one piece of independent writing from each pupil.
2 Identify all the spelling errors and record them on the grid. Decide what you think is the main source of the error and record the word in the corresponding column. It is a good idea to record the word as the pupil has spelt it.
3 Identify any patterns. Quite quickly you will be able to see which aspect of spelling needs to be addressed.

The headings on the grid included are

- Common exception words
- GPCs (grapheme–phoneme correspondences) including rarer GPCs and vowel digraphs
- Homophones
- Prefixes and suffixes
- Word endings
- Other.

These headings correspond to key strands within the National Curriculum. These could be changed or further areas added if needed.

Year					
Common exception words	GPC (includes rare GPCs and vowel digraphs)	Homophones	Prefixes and suffixes	Word endings	Others
firend whent	perants ~~for~~ Clouser (closer) flow (flew) amzing nealy eaven	their (there) x 2 .	phond horrerfied		~~orgument~~ argement

Complementary resources

To support the teaching, additional resources are recommended and referred to throughout the programme.

Spelling journals	Developing the use of spelling journals can support both teachers and pupils in many ways. They enable • pupils to take responsibility for their spelling learning • pupils to refer back to previous learning • teachers to see how pupils are tackling tricky bits of spelling • teachers and pupils to discuss spelling with parents and carers Spelling journals can take many forms and are much more than just a word book. Spelling journals can be used for • practising strategies • learning words • recording rules/conventions/ generalisations as an aide-memoire • word lists of really tricky words (spelling enemies) • 'Having a go' at the point of writing • ongoing record of statutory words learnt • investigations • recording spelling targets or goals • spelling tests. In the programme, there is flexibility for journals to be set up in a variety of ways. Below are a few recommendations: • Make sure that the journal can be used flexibly. A blank exercise book gives much more scope for pupils to try out ideas and organise their learning than a heavily structured format. • Model different ways of using the journal. A class spelling journal or examples from different pupils could be used to do this. • Give time for pupils to use their journals and to review them. • Do the majority of spelling work in the journal.

Have a go sheets	These are a key component of Strategies at the point of writing. They are introduced in the Year 2 programme and then revisited in Years 3, 4, 5 and 6. Schools need to decide how Have a go will form part of their spelling policy, together with the use of spelling journals and establishing routines for attempting unknown spellings. A Have a go sheet template is provided in the Supporting Resources. Have a go sheets can take several different forms, for example: • a large sheet of paper on a table that pupils write on when they need to. • sheets stuck in all pupils' books that fold out when pupils are writing • a book placed on the table open at a clean sheet for pupils to use. • a page in pupils' spelling journals. **Note:** it is important that teachers have an enlarged version of a Have a go sheet displayed for modelling when writing in any curriculum area and at any time in the school day. Introducing Have a Go: 1. Model writing a sentence and being unsure about how to spell a word. Talk about the tricky part in the word and some of the choices you might have for that part. You could refer to a GPC chart to find the choices if appropriate. 2. Model writing the word with two or three choices on your own enlarged version of a Have a go sheet and then model choosing the one that you think looks right and using it in your sentence. It is important that pupils learn to ask themselves the question 'Does it look right?' or 'Have I seen it like this in a book?' to help them make their choices. 3. If you are still unsure of the spelling, put a wiggly line under it in the sentence to signal that this needs checking by the teacher, or the pupil if appropriate, during proofreading time. 4. Model continuing with writing and *not* checking the correct version of the spelling at this point. This is important so that the flow of writing is not unnecessarily slowed. 5. Make sure you model this process briefly in writing in all curriculum areas. 6. Pupils use their own Have a Go sheet (or group sheet) whenever they write and refer to GPC charts and other classroom displays as support, as well as specific strategies that have been taught for using at the point of writing. 7. Remind them never to make more than three attempts at a word. Misspelt words will need to be corrected in line with your school's spelling and marking policy. Some of these words may be included in pupils' individual word lists for learning. To see lessons where Have a go strategies are first introduced, please refer to Year 2 Block 1 Lessons 11 and 17.
GPC (grapheme-phoneme correspondence) choices chart	The teaching of spelling complements very much the teaching of phonics. It is anticipated that the school will draw upon the GPC charts used in their phonics programme to work alongside the teaching of spelling.

Individual whiteboards	Individual whiteboards these can be used in a variety of ways to support lessons including checking spelling attempts, Quickwrite and Have a go.
Working wall	It is really useful to have a small area of display space in the classroom that can reflect current teaching focuses and provide support for pupils' spelling as they write. GPC charts, reminders of common spelling patterns or conventions and tricky words to remember could be part of a working wall for spelling.

Learning spellings

A school policy can help inform

- the strategies for learning spellings that are being taught
- routines for learning spellings
- links with home learning.

Learning needs to happen in school and at home. There is little evidence, though, that the traditional practice of learning spellings (usually 10) at home and being tested on them (usually on a Friday) is effective. However, there is a high expectation within the new National Curriculum that pupils will learn many increasingly complex words. Within the programme, learning spellings is built into each six-week block. Within the sessions a range of strategies for learning spellings are introduced and practised. This enables pupils to choose the strategies they find most effective for learning different words.

Tips for learning spellings at home

Learning at home needs to be an extension of the practice in school. Consider

- limiting the number of words to five or less a week to ensure success and enable deeper learning
- making sure pupils and parents have access to the range of learning strategies which have been taught in school, to use in home learning
- assessing spellings in context, for example: learning spellings in a given sentence, generating sentences for each word, assessing through unseen dictated sentences
- keeping an ongoing record of words learnt and setting very high expectations of correct application in writing once a word has been learned.

The learning strategies on the next two pages are introduced incrementally throughout the programme and can then be used to support learning spellings at home.

Look, say, cover, write, check	This is probably the most common strategy used to learn spellings. **Look**: first look at the whole word carefully and if there is one part of the word that is difficult, look at that part in more detail. **Say**: say the word as you look at it, using different ways of pronouncing it if that will make it more memorable. **Cover**: cover the word. **Write**: write the word from memory, saying the word as you do so. **Check**: Have you got it right? If yes, try writing it again and again! If not, start again – look, say, cover, write, check.
Trace, copy and replicate (and then check)	This is a similar learning process to 'look, say, cover, write, check' but is about developing automaticity and muscle memory. Write the word out on a sheet of paper ensuring that it is spelt correctly and it is large enough to trace over. Trace over the word and say it at the same time. Move next to the word you have just written and write it out as you say it. Turn the page over and write the word as you say it, and then check that you have spelt it correctly. If this is easy, do the same process for two different words at the same time. Once you have written all your words this way and feel confident, miss out the tracing and copying or the tracing alone and just write the words.
Segmentation strategy	The splitting of a word into its constituent phonemes in the correct order to support spelling.
Quickwrite	Writing the words linked to the teaching focus with speed and fluency. The aim is to write as many words as possible within a time constraint. Pupils can write words provided by the teacher or generate their own examples. For example, in two minutes write as many words as possible with the /iː/ phoneme. This can be turned into a variety of competitive games including working in teams and developing relay race approaches.
Drawing around the word to show the shape	Draw around the words making a clear distinction in size where there are ascenders and descenders. Look carefully at the shape of the word and the letters in each box. Now try to write the word making sure that you get the same shape. t o t a l l y

Drawing an image around the word	This strategy is all about making a word memorable. It links to meaning in order to try to make the spelling noticeable. You can't use this method as your main method of learning spellings, but it might work on those that are just a little more difficult to remember.
Words without vowels	This strategy is useful where the vowel choices are the challenge in the words. Write the words without the vowels and pupils have to choose the correct grapheme to put in the space. For example, for the word *field*: f____ld
Pyramid words	This method of learning words forces you to think of each letter separately. p p y p y r p y r a p y r a m p y r a m i p y r a m i d You can then reverse the process so that you end up with a diamond.
Other strategies	Other methods can include: • Rainbow writing. Using coloured pencils in different ways can help to make parts of words memorable. You could highlight the tricky parts of the word or write the tricky part in a different colour. You could also write each letter in a different colour, or write the word in red, then overlay in orange, yellow and so on. • Making up memorable 'silly sentences' containing the word • Saying the word in a funny way – for example, pronouncing the 'silent' letters in a word • Clapping and counting to identify the syllables in a word.

Year 2 National Curriculum requirements

Pupils should be taught to

- develop a range of personal strategies for learning new and irregular words*
- develop a range of personal strategies for spelling at the point of composition*
- develop a range of strategies for checking and proofreading spellings after writing*

Pupils should be taught to spell by

- segmenting spoken words into phonemes and representing these by graphemes, spelling many correctly
- learning new ways of spelling phonemes for which one or more spellings are already known, and learning some words with each spelling, including a few common homophones
- learning to spell common exception words
- learning to spell more words with contracted forms
- learning the possessive apostrophe (singular), for example, the girl's book
- distinguishing between homophones and near homophones
- adding suffixes to spell longer words, for example, '-ment', '-ful', '-less', '-ly'
- applying spelling rules and guidelines, as listed in English Appendix 1
- writing from memory simple sentences dictated by the teacher that include words using the GPCs, common exception words and punctuation taught so far.

* non-statutory

Year 2 lesson plans

Year 2 Term 1 overview

Block 1 – autumn first half term

Week 1	Lesson 1 Revise/Teach/Practise/Apply **Phase 5 GPCs including polysyllabic words. Homophones (*sea/see* and *be/bee*)**	Lesson 2 Teach **Strategies at the point of writing: using a GPC chart**	Lesson 3 Practise **Phase 5 GPCs**	Lesson 4 Teach **Strategies for learning words: using spelling journals**	Lesson 5 Practise **Using segmentation strategy for learning selected words**
Week 2	Lesson 6 Revise/Teach/Practise/Apply **Phase 5 GPCs Homophones (*blue/blew*)**	Lesson 7 Revise/Teach/Practise/Apply **Phase 5 GPCs and relevant homophones.**	Lesson 8 Teach **Strategies at the point of writing: using the environment**	Lesson 9 Practise **Using segmentation and Phase 5 GPCs to learn words from this week**	Lesson 10 Assess **Selected Phase 5 GPCs and homophones: dictation**
Week 3	Lesson 11 Teach **Strategies at the point of writing: Have a go sheets**	Lesson 12 Revise/Teach/Practise/Apply **Phase 5 GPCs and homophones**	Lesson 13 Revise/Teach/Practise/Apply **Phase 5 GPCs and homophones**	Lesson 14 Teach **Strategies for learning words: highlighting the tricky part in common exception words**	Lesson 15 Practise **Words learnt this week: common exception words and Phase 5 GPCs**
Week 4	Lesson 16 Revise/Teach/Practise/Apply **Phase 5 GPCs including polysyllabic words**	Lesson 17 Revise **Strategies at the point of writing: Have a go sheets**	Lesson 18 Teach/Practise/Apply **Proofreading: using word banks for common exception words**	Lesson 19 Learn **Strategies for learning words: polysyllabic and common exception words**	Lesson 20 Apply **Strategies for learning words: polysyllabic and common exception words**
Week 5	Lesson 21 Teach/Practise/Apply **Proofreading, especially high-frequency words**	Lesson 22 Teach **Homophones**	Lesson 23 Teach **Strategies for learning words: tricky parts of words and Look, say, cover, write, check**	Lesson 24 Revise/Learn **Strategies for learning words: Look, say, cover, write, check**	Lesson 25 Apply **Homophones learnt so far**
Week 6	Lesson 26 Revise **/aɪ/ spelt 'i' in common exception words (*find, kind, mind, behind, child, wild, climb*)**	Lesson 27 Practise **/aɪ/ spelt 'i' in common exception words (*find, kind, mind, behind, child, wild, climb*)**	Lesson 28 Revise/Practise **Strategies for learning words: selected words from personal lists**	Lesson 29 Learn **Strategies for learning words: words from this half term**	Lesson 30 Assess **Words from this half term**

No Nonsense Spelling

Block 2 – autumn second half term

Week 1	Lesson 1 Teach/Practise/Apply **Strategies for learning words: Look, say, cover, write, check for common exception words**	Lesson 2 Teach **Strategies for learning words: kinaesthetic and visual strategies for learning common exception words**	Lesson 3 Teach/Practise **Proofreading common exception words and high-frequency words**	Lesson 4 Practise **Strategies for learning words: common exception words and personal words**	Lesson 5 Apply **Common exception words and personal words: dictation**
Week 2	Lesson 6 Revise **Phase 5 GPCs that are not secure**	Lesson 7 Teach **Homophones (to/two/too)**	Lesson 8 Revise/Teach/Apply **Homophones (to/two/too)**	Lesson 9 Revise **Strategies at the point of writing: Have a go**	Lesson 10 Apply **Strategies for learning words: Rainbow write**
Week 3	Lesson 11 Revise **Selected Phase 5 GPCs**	Lesson 12 Teach **Strategies at the point of writing: Word sort**	Lesson 13 Revise/Teach/Practise: **Strategies at the point of writing: Have a go**	Lesson 14 Practise: **Strategies at the point of writing: Which one looks right?**	Lesson 15 Learn **Strategies for learning words: selected topic words for this term**
Week 4	Lesson 16 Revise **/dʒ/ sound spelt as 'ge' and 'dge' at the end of words, and sometimes as 'g' elsewhere in words before 'e', 'i' and 'y'**	Lesson 17 Practise **/dʒ/ sound spelt as 'ge' and 'dge' at the end of words, and sometimes as 'g' elsewhere in words before 'e', 'i' and 'y'**	Lesson 18 Teach/Practise **Proofreading: using the environment and the working wall**	Lesson 19 Apply **/dʒ/ sound spelt as 'ge' and 'dge' at the end of words, and sometimes as 'g' elsewhere in words before 'e', 'i' and 'y'**	Lesson 20 Practise **Strategies for learning words: selected spellings from personal lists, common errors and /dʒ/ words**
Week 5	Lesson 21 Teach **/s/ sound spelt 'c' before 'e', 'i' and 'y'**	Lesson 22 Practise **/s/ sound spelt 'c' before 'e', 'i' and 'y'**	Lesson 23 Apply **/s/ sound spelt 'c' before 'e', 'i' and 'y': dictation**	Lesson 24 Teach/Revise **Homophones (here/hear, one/won, sun/son)** **Revise homophones taught so far**	Lesson 25 Practise/Apply **Homophones (here/hear, one/won, sun/son)** **Revise homophones taught so far**
Week 6	Lesson 26 Revise **/n/ sound spelt 'kn' and 'gn' at the beginning of words**	Lesson 27 Practise **/n/ sound spelt 'kn' and 'gn' at the beginning of words**	Lesson 28 Teach **Strategies for learning words: saying the word in a funny way**	Lesson 29 Learn **Strategies for learning words: saying the word in a funny way**	Lesson 30 Assess **/n/ sound spelt 'kn' and 'gn' at the beginning of words: dictation**

Block 1 – autumn first half term

Lesson	Year 2, block 1, lesson 1
Lesson type	Revise/Teach/Practise/Apply
Lesson focus	**Phase 5 GPCs** **Homophones (*sea/see* and *be/bee*)**
Resources needed	Supporting Resources 2.3 (GPC chart), 2.4 (image and word cards for homophones)
Teaching activity	Revise any Phase 5 sounds (from Letters and Sounds or your equivalent phonics scheme) that pupils are not secure with. Teach a lesson based around these using segmentation to match each phoneme to a grapheme. Include relevant homophones for your chosen phoneme. For example, use this lesson when revising the /ee/ phoneme. Refer to your phonics scheme for ideas and activities, for example: • Introduce pupils to the idea that there are some words that sound the same but are spelt differently. • Write up the words *sea* and *see* on the board. • Add sound buttons and talk about the different ways of writing the sound /ee/. Show pupils the images that match the words and ask them to link the word to the image. Introduce *be* and *bee* in a similar way. Demonstrate handwriting for each word in turn. Pupils can practise alongside you in their spelling journals. Dictate the following sentences for pupils to write, spelling all the words correctly. Pupils should include punctuation in the sentences. *I can see the sea.* *Can you see me?* *The sea is grey today.*

Lesson	Year 2, block 1, lesson 2
Lesson type	Teach
Lesson focus	**Strategies at the point of writing: using a GPC chart**
Resources needed	Supporting Resource 2.3 (GPC chart)
Teaching activity	Display a large GPC chart and teach pupils how to find their way around it. Focus on GPCs that pupils are familiar with and have been revising this week. Give out individual charts and display some Phase 5 words. Ask pupils to locate where those words would fit on the chart. What other spellings can they see for that phoneme?

Block 1 – autumn first half term

Lesson	Year 2, block 1, lesson 3
Lesson type	Practise
Lesson focus	**Phase 5 GPCs**
Resources needed	Supporting Resource 2.3 (GPC chart)
Teaching activity	Play 'Words without vowels'. Display a word from those practised this week with the focus grapheme missing. Ask pupils to try writing the word, choosing from the choices on the chart, for example, st__p. Choices are ea/ee/ey. Which one looks right? Model writing a sentence and attempting to spell a word with an appropriate grapheme using the GPC chart.

Lesson	Year 2, block 1, lesson 4
Lesson type	Teach
Lesson focus	**Strategies for learning words: using spelling journals**
Resources needed	Spelling journals
Teaching activity	Introduce spelling journals (see page 7) and explain their purpose. Model writing words from this week and using segmentation strategies to match each phoneme to a grapheme.

Lesson	Year 2, block 1, lesson 5
Lesson type	Practise
Lesson focus	**Using segmentation strategy for learning selected words**
Resources needed	Spelling journals
Teaching activity	Provide pupils with a small selection of words to learn either from the common exception words for Year 2 (page 79), words that pupils are commonly spelling incorrectly, or words containing GPCs that you have looked at in previous sessions. Pupils practise using segmentation strategy to learn the words.

Block 1 – autumn first half term

Lesson	Year 2, block 1, lesson 6
Lesson type	Revise/Teach/Practise/Apply
Lesson focus	**Phase 5 GPCs** **Homophones (blue/blew)**
Resources needed	Supporting Resource 2.4 (Image and word cards for homophones), spelling journals, GPC wall chart
Teaching activity	Revise any Phase 5 sounds that pupils are not secure with and teach a lesson based around these using segmentation to match each phoneme to a grapheme. Include relevant homophones for your chosen phoneme. For example, use this lesson when revising the /ʊ/ phoneme. Review what the pupils know about homophones and remind them about *sea* and *see*. Tell pupils that there are other words like *sea* and *see*. Ask them to do the following: • Look at the pictures in the resource and try to identify the homophones. • Sound out the words and clap for the phonemes. • Think about different ways the sound /ew/ can be spelt. • Refer to the GPC wall chart to support looking at the choices. Give pupils cards for the *blew* and *blue* images and read out the following sentences. Pupils hold up the correct image card. *The wind blew and blew.* *Blue is my favourite colour.* *The sky is very blue.* *I blew the balloons up.* Do this again but this time ask pupils to write the word. Use Quickwrite for *blue/blew* after saying the sentence *I blew my nose*. Pupils Quickwrite *blew* for two minutes and then check. Repeat with the sentence *My bruise is black and blue*. Pupils add relevant words to their spelling journals to learn.

Lesson	Year 2, block 1, lesson 7
Lesson type	Revise/Teach/Practise/Apply
Lesson focus	**Phase 5 GPCs and relevant homophones**
Resources needed	Supporting Resource 2.4 (Image and word cards for homophones), spelling journals
Teaching activity	Continue to revise any Phase 5 sounds that pupils are not secure with. Teach a lesson based around them using segmentation to match each phoneme to a grapheme. Include relevant homophones.

Block 1 – autumn first half term

Lesson	Year 2, block 1, lesson 8
Lesson type	Teach
Lesson focus	**Strategies at the point of writing: using the environment**
Resources needed	GPC charts, selected words for display around classroom
Teaching activity	Display around the room words with Phase 5 GPCs that pupils are learning. These could be on the wall or on tables. Model writing and using the displayed words. Teach pupils how to hold a letter or more than one letter in their heads when copying. Establish expectations and 'non-negotiables' for spelling displayed words correctly. You might say that copied words must always be spelt correctly and call this a 'non-negotiable'. Ensure that each time pupils write during the day they use their GPC charts and the supports around the room.

Lesson	Year 2, block 1, lesson 9
Lesson type	Practise
Lesson focus	**Using segmentation and Phase 5 GPCs to learn words from this week**
Resources needed	GPC chart, spelling journals
Teaching activity	Model how to learn words from this week using segmentation and by matching each phoneme to a corresponding grapheme. Ask pupils to practise with words in their spelling journals. Can they write all their words correctly?

Lesson	Year 2, block 1, lesson 10
Lesson type	Assess
Lesson focus	**Selected Phase 5 GPCs and homophones: dictation**
Resources needed	Spelling journals
Teaching activity	Dictate sentences with the relevant Phase 5 GPCs and homophones. Check the sentences with pupils. Which words are they still finding tricky? Display those words on the wall with the tricky part highlighted. Pupils should practise saying the words letter by letter.

Block 1 – autumn first half term

Lesson	Year 2, block 1, lesson 11
Lesson type	Teach
Lesson focus	**Strategies at the point of writing: Have a go sheets**
Resources needed	Supporting Resource 2.2 (Have a go sheet)
Teaching activity	This session is all about setting up Have a go sheets. These can take several forms: • A large sheet of paper on a table that pupils just write on when they need to. • Sheets stuck in a book that fold out when pupils are writing • A book placed on the table open at a clean sheet for all pupils to use. • A page in pupils' spelling journals Model writing a sentence and being unsure how to spell a word. Talk about the tricky part in the word and some of the choices you might have for that part. Try writing the word with two or three of the choices, but not more than three, and then model choosing the one that you think looks right and using it in your sentence. If you are still unsure of the spelling, put a wiggly line under it in the sentence to signal that this needs checking by the teacher or pupil (if appropriate). Make sure you model doing this every time you write in all curriculum areas. Pupils use their own Have a go sheet (or group sheet) whenever they write. Remind them only to make two or three attempts at a word and then to make a choice and continue writing. They do not check whether the word is correct at this point. Misspelt words will need to be corrected in line with your school's spelling and marking policy. Some of these words may be included in pupils' individual word lists for learning. Write these steps you have modelled in the lesson as a simple sheet to be stuck onto the pupils' writing books and spelling journals. This will become the prompt and reminder about what to do when they come to a word they don't know how to spell at the point of writing.

Block 1 – autumn first half term

Lesson	Year 2, block 1, lessons 12 and 13
Lesson type	Revise/Teach/Practise/Apply
Lesson focus	**Phase 5 GPCs and homophones**
Resources needed	Supporting Resource 2.4 (Image and word cards for homophones), spelling journals
Teaching activity	Revise any Phase 5 sounds that pupils are not secure with and teach a lesson based around these, using segmentation to match each phoneme to a grapheme. Include relevant homophones. Refer to your phonics scheme for ideas and activities, for example: • Use pictures of homophones, for example, a flower and some flour. • Get pupils to have a go at writing the words. • Discuss the tricky bits of the words and highlight them. • Practise handwriting the words and link to other words with similar spellings of the sound, for example, *The hour hand on the clock points to three.* Use Quickwrite for all three words. Add any relevant words to spelling journals to learn. In the second lesson, continue revising any Phase 5 sounds that pupils are not secure with and teach a lesson based around these using segmentation to match each phoneme to a grapheme. Include relevant homophones.

Lesson	Year 2, block 1, lesson 14
Lesson type	Teach
Lesson focus	**Strategies for learning words: highlighting the tricky part in selected common exception words**
Resources needed	Common exception words for Year 2 (page 79), spelling journals
Teaching activity	Explain to pupils that they are going to improve their spelling by being able to identify the tricky parts in words. Choose common exception words or words that pupils have not spelt correctly in their writing. Say the first word for pupils to write in their spelling journals and ask them to underline any part of the word they find difficult. Discuss why these parts were tricky. Put some of the possible spellings on the board including the correct spelling. Discuss the fact that some of the words might be correct phonically but may be pronounced differently. Focus on the correct spelling by rubbing out the others, underlining or highlighting the tricky bit and talking about why it is tricky. Agree a way of recalling the word in the future such as closing your eyes and 'seeing' the highlighted part. Cover the word and ask pupils to write it in their journals again and compare it with the original. Have they spelt it correctly this time? Do they understand why they haven't spelt it correctly? Do they have a strategy for remembering it? Repeat for other words.

Block 1 – autumn first half term

Lesson	Year 2, block 1, lesson 15
Lesson type	Practise
Lesson focus	**Words learnt this week: common exception words and Phase 5 GPCs**
Resources needed	Spelling journals
Teaching activity	Model taking several words recorded in pupils' spelling journals this week and writing them into a silly sentence which is grammatically accurate but doesn't make sense. For example, *The rabbit ate the gentleman for tea.* Reinforce capital letters and full stops, question marks or exclamation marks. Pupils write their own spelling journal words in silly sentences focusing on spelling those words correctly.

Lesson	Year 2, block 1, lesson 16
Lesson type	Revise/Teach/Practise/Apply
Lesson focus	**Phase 5 GPCs including polysyllabic words**
Resources needed	Spelling journals
Teaching activity	Revise any Phase 5 sounds, particularly in polysyllabic words, and teach a lesson based around these, using syllables as a strategy for helping with spelling. Explain that some words have more than one syllable, or beat, and we can find those out by clapping and counting as we say the word. Try clapping out pupils' names. Choose words of more than one syllable, for example, *donkey, football, sadly*, that relate to the GPCs that pupils need to revise. Say a word. Pupils clap it out and then write each syllable in a box. Discuss the choices that pupils might have to make and where they can find support for this in the room. Call out a polysyllabic word. Pupils work in pairs to count the syllables and then hold up their fingers to show the number. Clap and count the syllables together. Pupils add any relevant words to their spelling journals.

Block 1 – autumn first half term

Lesson	Year 2, block 1, lesson 17
Lesson type	Revise
Lesson focus	**Strategies at the point of writing: Have a go sheets**
Resources needed	Have a go sheets
Teaching activity	Revise using Have a go sheets when writing. Remind pupils about the strategies they have learnt so far for having a go: • Using a GPC chart • Using spellings that are in the environment • Segmenting and matching phoneme to grapheme • Chunking words into syllables Ask pupils to write a sentence linked to something they have done this week. Ask them to use their strategies to have a go at any unknown spellings and to use a wiggly line if they are still not sure.

Lesson	Year 2, block 1, lesson 18
Lesson type	Teach/Practise/Apply
Lesson focus	**Proofreading: using word banks for common exception words**
Resources needed	Common exception words for Year 2 (page 79), spelling journals, examples of the pupils' own writing.
Teaching activity	Display the common exception words on the wall. Only include those that pupils are not spelling correctly in their writing. Choose three or four of the common exception words that appear in most writing – for example, *some, come, here, there, friend*. Put them on the board. Look at each word and identify the tricky part of the word. Draw around it. Show that this word is displayed on the wall. Put a range of sentences from pupils' writing on the board with these words spelt incorrectly. Model reading through one carefully and identifying the incorrect spelling and changing it, referring to the word bank on the wall. Revise non-negotiables for spelling displayed words correctly. Pupils work through the rest of the sentences, spotting the errors and changing them. Pupils look through their own writing and check that these words are spelt correctly. It might help if you have placed a star by a sentences in their books that they need to check. Pupils add any relevant words to their spelling journals.

Block 1 – autumn first half term

Lesson	Year 2, block 1, lesson 19
Lesson type	Learn
Lesson focus	**Strategies for learning words: polysyllabic and common exception words**
Resources needed	Supporting Resource 2.3 (GPC chart), spelling journals
Teaching activity	Revise using syllable strategy to help pupils learn Phase 5 polysyllabic words in spelling journals. Model highlighting the tricky bit for common exception words. Pupils learn their word lists and practise writing the words.

Lesson	Year 2, block 1, lesson 20
Lesson type	Apply
Lesson focus	**Strategies for learning words: polysyllabic and common exception words**
Resources needed	Spelling journals
Teaching activity	Read the polysyllabic words and common exception words practised this week in sentences. Pupils write the focus words. Check the words together. Which ones are still tricky? What could we do to help remember them?

Lesson	Year 2, block 1, lesson 21
Lesson type	Teach/Practise/Apply
Lesson focus	**Proofreading, especially high-frequency words**
Resources needed	Spelling journals
Teaching activity	Ensure each pupil has a spelling partner. Put up a few sentences on the board with spelling errors in high-frequency words, plus any sentences from the previous lesson that had spelling errors in them. Model reading through the sentences, looking for errors and words with wiggly lines and correcting them. Pupils use their spelling journals and the environment to support their decision making. Teach pupils how to copy words correctly by looking up and memorising each part of the word. Spelling partners continue working through the examples on the board. Spelling partners read through sentences, possibly from their own writing, to find and correct errors. It might help if you have placed a star by a sentence in their books that they need to check. Pupils add words to their spelling journals.

No Nonsense Spelling

Block 1 – autumn first half term

Lesson	Year 2, block 1, lesson 22
Lesson type	Teach
Lesson focus	**Homophones**
Resources needed	Supporting Resource 2.4 (image and word cards for homophones), spelling journals
Teaching activity	Share all the images with the pupils showing all the homophones used so far, including *whole* and *hole*. Use the word cards and match the word to the image ensuring that you use the correct spelling. Pupils then continue this activity in pairs. Extend the activity for some by asking them to make up sentences using the words and write them in their spelling journals. Pupils add relevant words to their spelling journals.

Lesson	Year 2, block 1, lesson 23
Lesson type	Teach
Lesson focus	**Strategies for learning words: tricky parts of words and Look, say, cover, write, check**
Resources needed	Spelling journals
Teaching activity	Remind pupils of the strategy of highlighting tricky parts of words. Introduce the word *beautiful*. Clap out the syllables and separate the word out into its syllables: *beau-ti-ful*. Discuss how to remember the tricky parts of each syllable. Look at the word, say the word, cover the word and write it. Check whether pupils have spelt it correctly. Pupils practise handwriting the tricky parts of *beautiful*.

Lesson	Year 2, block 1, lesson 24
Lesson type	Revise/Learn
Lesson focus	**Strategies for learning words: Look, say, cover, write, check**
Resources needed	Spelling journals
Teaching activity	Before this session, ensure that you have looked through pupils' spelling journals and written in any words that they didn't get correct on their Have a go sheets. Pupils choose 3–5 of these words to learn *or* you can choose words from this week's sessions. Revise the Look, say, cover, write, check strategy for learning words by working on a couple of words together. Ask pupils to find the words that they need to learn and use Look, say, cover, write, check on each one in their spelling journals.

Block 1 – autumn first half term

Lesson	Year 2, block 1, lesson 25
Lesson type	Apply
Lesson focus	**Homophones learnt so far**
Resources needed	Supporting Resource 2.4 (image and word cards for homophones)
Teaching activity	Show one of the homophone images and create a sentence around it, for example, *I can **see** a dog*. Pupils write the sentence, using a capital letter and full stop. Pupils then check a partner's spelling. Do this for all the homophones (or as many as you can in the time).

Lesson	Year 2, block 1, lesson 26
Lesson type	Revise
Lesson focus	/aɪ/ **spelt 'i' in common exception words (*find, kind, mind, behind, child, wild, climb*)**
Resources needed	Spelling journals
Teaching activity	Model how to use analogy to spell these words. Put one word up on the board, for example, *mind*. Pupils sound it out and think about the alternative pronunciations for the letter 'i'. Explain to pupils that if they know how to spell *mind*, they can spell other words like it. Get the pupils to practise handwriting the word *mind*. Can pupils use this word to help them spell *kind, find, wild, child, behind*? They write each word in their spelling journals and check that the correct spelling has been used.

Lesson	Year 2, block 1, lesson 27
Lesson type	Practise
Lesson focus	/aɪ/ **sound spelt 'i' in common exception words (*find, kind, mind, behind, child, wild, climb*)**
Resources needed	Supporting Resource 2.5 (wordsearch)
Teaching activity	Use the wordsearch provided with the target words hidden. How many words can the pupils find and write out correctly? There are seven words. (Answers: *find, kind, mind, behind, child, wild, climb*)

Block 1 – autumn first half term

Lesson	Year 2, block 1, lesson 28
Lesson type	Revise/Practise
Lesson focus	**Strategies for learning words: selected words from personal lists**
Resources needed	Spelling journals
Teaching activity	Revise the strategies the pupils have learnt this half term to learn the spellings of words. Practise some of these strategies on words from their spelling journals.

Lesson	Year 2, block 1, lesson 29
Lesson type	Learn
Lesson focus	**Strategies for learning words: words from this half term**
Resources needed	Spelling journals
Teaching activity	Pupils use a favourite strategy for learning words from this half term.

Lesson	Year 2, block 1, lesson 30
Lesson type	Assess
Lesson focus	**Words from this half term**
Resources needed	(Various, see activities below)
Teaching activity	Play games to assess words learnt this half term. For example: • Hold up homophone pictures and ask pupils to write the words. • Dictate a sentence with two or three known words in it. • Get pupils to look at a word spelt in different ways on the board and choose the correct one.

Block 2 – autumn second half term

Lesson	Year 2, block 2, lesson 1
Lesson type	Teach/Practise/Apply
Lesson focus	**Strategies for learning words: Look, say, cover, write, check for common exception words**
Resources needed	Common exception words for Year 2 (page 79), spelling journals
Teaching activity	Pupils work in their spelling journals. Choose a common exception word that many pupils don't spell correctly in their writing and write it on the board. Model how to look closely at it, identify the tricky part and highlight it. Tell pupils to take a 'photograph' of the word with their eyes to try and remember it. They should say the word as they look at it. Cover up the word and ask pupils to write it from memory. Uncover the word and check it. Is it right? Is there still a bit that needs to be remembered? How could you remember it? Try again. Take pupils through the selected words one at a time. Ask pupils to choose one word of their own that they want to spell correctly and do 'Look, say, cover, write, check' on it. Pupils add the words to their spelling journals.

Lesson	Year 2, block 2, lesson 2
Lesson type	Teach
Lesson focus	**Strategies for learning words: kinaesthetic and visual strategies for learning common exception words**
Resources needed	On tables: sand tray, marker pens, play dough etc, spelling journals
Teaching activity	Using the common exception words from the previous lesson, teach the pupils how to memorise them by practising handwriting them: • in the air – with one hand, both hands, little finger, foot • on their partner's back with their finger • on the palm of their hand • in sand trays, with play dough etc. Consolidate by getting pupils to write the words in their spelling journals. How did this activity help them remember the spellings?

No Nonsense Spelling

Block 2 – autumn second half term

Lesson	Year 2, block 2, lesson 3
Lesson type	Teach/Practise
Lesson focus	**Proofreading common exception words and high-frequency words**
Resources needed	Common exception words for Year 2 (page 79), spelling journals, rulers, examples of pupils' own writing
Teaching activity	Model using several sentences with errors and a ruler or piece of paper to isolate one line at a time. Model finding errors. Teach pupils to find the words in a word bank or another place in the environment. Correct the words. Pupils use the same process for their own writing and choose two or three words to add to their spelling journals to learn.

Lesson	Year 2, block 2, lesson 4
Lesson type	Practise
Lesson focus	**Strategies for learning words: common exception words and personal words**
Resources needed	Common exception words for Year 2 (page 79), spelling journals
Teaching activity	Pupils use strategies learnt this week to learn common exception words and words from their writing. Pupils use Quickwrite to consolidate their learning.

Lesson	Year 2, block 2, lesson 5
Lesson type	Apply
Lesson focus	**Common exception words and personal words: dictation**
Resources needed	Common exception words for Year 2 (page 79), spelling journals
Teaching activity	Dictate sentences using the common exception words from this week. Ask pupils to write another sentence with at least one of their own words in it.

Lesson	Year 2, block 2, lesson 6
Lesson type	Revise
Lesson focus	**Phase 5 GPCs that are not secure**
Resources needed	Spelling journals
Teaching activity	Choose any Phase 5 GPCs that pupils are not secure with and teach a lesson based around these. Use key activities from other sessions. Pupils add relevant words to their spelling journals.

Block 2 – autumn second half term

Lesson	Year 2, block 2, lesson 7
Lesson type	Teach
Lesson focus	**Homophones (*to*/*two*/*too*)**
Resources needed	Chalk, outside space
Teaching activity	Display the three target words and ask pupils to read them. Does anyone know the difference between the words? Choose the word *two* and talk about the fact that it is a number. What do we call two pupils who are born at the same time? (*twins*) If something happens two times we say *twice*. We also have the numbers *twelve* and *twenty*. Write all these words on the board and show the link with the number 2 and the spelling *two*. In the playground, chalk the words *two* and *to* several times. Read out the following sentences and ask pupils to go and stand on the correct word. They come back to stand near you after each sentence. *I have two sisters.* *I am going to the park.* *Go to the hall.* *I am looking forward to going on holiday.* *I bought two apples today.*

Lesson	Year 2, block 2, lesson 8
Lesson type	Revise/Teach/Apply
Lesson focus	**Homophones (*to*/*two*/*too*)**
Resources needed	Supporting Resource 2.6 (cards with *two*, *to* and *too*)
Teaching activity	Revise *to* and *two* from the previous session by playing the outdoor game again. Explain to pupils that there is another word *too* which means 'excessive' or 'also'. We use it when we say something or someone is *too* hot, *too* cold, *too* busy, to show that it is *too* much! Pupils practise handwriting the word *too*. Pupils orally create sentences using *too*. In pairs, pupils have cards with *two*, *to* and *too* on them. Read out the sentences below and ask pupils to decide which card should be held up. Discuss for each sentence why they have chosen the card they have held up. *The other day I went to the post office.* *While I was there I bought a shirt and two pairs of shoes.* *I went to the cash register to pay and to have the items put in a bag.* *As I was leaving the store, the bag broke open because it was too thin.*

Block 2 – autumn second half term

Lesson	Year 2, block 2, lesson 9
Lesson type	Revise
Lesson focus	**Strategies at the point of writing: Have a go**
Resources needed	GPC charts
Teaching activity	Remind pupils of the Have a go strategy. Show a word with gaps and ask pupils to think what letters could go in the gap to make a word. Give them alternatives if necessary or ask them to look at GPC charts and try some out – for example, p____k h_____d d_____r Get the pupils to check the words by asking 'Does it look right?' Decide on the correct spellings and ways to learn the ones that were tricky.

Lesson	Year 2, block 2, lesson 10
Lesson type	Apply
Lesson focus	**Strategies for learning words: Rainbow write**
Resources needed	Selection of the pupils' topic words
Teaching activity	Prepare a selection of the pupils' topic words. Ask the pupils which words will be tricky to learn and which are the tricky parts in those words. Choose two or three of the words for pupils to learn and Rainbow write these – write each word out in a different colour each time. Pupils practise handwriting the words.

Lesson	Year 2, block 2, lesson 11
Lesson type	Revise
Lesson focus	**Selected Phase 5 GPCs**
Resources needed	Supporting Resource 2.3 (GPC chart), spelling journals
Teaching activity	Revise any Phase 5 GPCs that pupils are not secure with and teach a lesson based around these and any relevant homophones, using activities and resources from previous lessons. Pupils add relevant words to their spelling journals.

Block 2 – autumn second half term

Lesson	Year 2, block 2, lesson 12
Lesson type	Teach
Lesson focus	**Strategies at the point of writing: Word sort**
Resources needed	Supporting Resource 2.3 (GPC chart)
Teaching activity	Prepare lists of words using any Phase 5 GPCs revised so far. Play 'Word sort' by sorting words into lists of the same spelling. Look at which is the most common spelling for each GPC. How could they use this new knowledge when 'having a go' in their writing? Make a display of the findings on the working wall.

Lesson	Year 2, block 2, lesson 13
Lesson type	Revise/Teach/Practise
Lesson focus	**Strategies at the point of writing: Have a go**
Resources needed	Supporting Resource 2.3 (GPC chart)
Teaching activity	Write up several versions of a word with different GPC possibilities including the correct one. Ask pupils which one looks right. Model choosing the correct one and writing it in a sentence. Refer back to the most common spelling for that GPC and making sensible choices. Get pupils to practise 'taking a photograph' with their eyes of the correct spelling, holding the image in their heads and writing the word down. Practise with another commonly misspelt word.

Lesson	Year 2, block 2, lesson 14
Lesson type	Practise
Lesson focus	**Strategies at the point of writing: Which one looks right?**
Resources needed	Spelling journals
Teaching activity	Play 'Which one looks right?' asking pupils to choose between different possible spellings of known words. Check pupils' decisions. Which ones are still tricky? Use Quickwrite to consolidate the correct spelling of tricky words.

Block 2 – autumn second half term

Lesson	Year 2, block 2, lesson 15
Lesson type	Learn
Lesson focus	**Strategies for learning words: selected topic words for this term**
Resources needed	Spelling journals
Teaching activity	Pupils recall the spelling strategies that they have used: • Highlighting tricky parts • Look, say, cover, write, check • Rainbow writing • Writing words in the air, etc. • Chunking words into syllables and then matching phonemes to graphemes Choose two or three topic words that pupils want to learn. They use their best strategies to learn the words.

Lesson	Year 2, block 2, lesson 16
Lesson type	Revise
Lesson focus	**/dʒ/ sound spelt as 'ge' and 'dge' at the end of words, and sometimes as 'g' elsewhere in words before 'e', 'i' and 'y'**
Resources needed	Supporting Resource 2.7 (blank and completed table)
Teaching activity	Ask pupils to give you words with the /dʒ/ sound in them. Record and categorise them in the blank table provided according to the way in which /dʒ/ is spelt. What do pupils notice about the sound, the different ways it is spelt and where they appear in a word? Are there any differences between the 'ge' and 'dge' columns? (The 'dge' column has short vowels.) Pupils say what they notice. As they do so, annotate a large version of this table for the wall. **Notes:** • The letter 'j' is never used for the /dʒ/ sound at the end of English words. • At the end of a word, the /dʒ/ sound is spelt '-dge' straight after the /æ/, /ɛ/, /ɪ/, /ɒ/, /ʌ/ and /ʊ/ sounds (sometimes called 'short' vowels). • After all other sounds, whether vowels or consonants, the /dʒ/ sound is spelt as '-ge' at the end of a word. • In other positions in words, the /dʒ/ sound is often (but not always) spelt as 'g' before 'e', 'i' and 'y'. • The /dʒ/ sound is always spelt as 'j' before 'a', 'o' and 'u'.

Block 2 – autumn second half term

Lesson	Year 2, block 2, lesson 17
Lesson type	Practise
Lesson focus	/dʒ/ **sound spelt as 'ge' and 'dge' at the end of words, and sometimes as 'g' elsewhere in words before 'e', 'i' and 'y'**
Resources needed	Supporting Resource 2.8 (images of /dʒ/ words), spelling journals
Teaching activity	Look back at the table from the previous lesson and ask pupils to share what they remember. Cover the words in the table but not the spellings and annotations and then show pupils a range of images for these words. Can they use the notes to work out how the /dʒ/ should be spelt? Pupils write the words in their spelling journals. Go through the spellings as a class for pupils to check their work.

Lesson	Year 2, block 2, lesson 18
Lesson type	Teach/Practise
Lesson focus	**Proofreading: using the environment and working wall**
Resources needed	Words on the classroom walls
Teaching activity	Read through all the words on the walls in the classroom that are there to help pupils. Have a couple of sentences from pupils' writing that have some of these words misspelt. Model reading though the sentences, identifying misspelt words, and using the wall/word bank/environment to find the correct spelling if you don't know it. Pupils work on one or two sentences in their own writing. It would help if you have placed a star by sentences that they need to look at.

Lesson	Year 2, block 2, lesson 19
Lesson type	Apply
Lesson focus	/dʒ/ **sound spelt as 'ge' and 'dge' at the end of words, and sometimes as 'g' elsewhere in words before 'e', 'i' and 'y'**
Resources needed	Supporting Resource 2.9 (word cards) and 2.7 (completed table), spelling journals
Teaching activity	Put the word cards into a pot and draw them out one at a time. Read out the word and pupils write it down. Include the new words *large*, *fridge* and *gentle* in the pot so that pupils have to think about them, not just remember the ones they have used previously. Add the new words to the table from Lesson 16. Pupils identify words to add to their personal learning lists.

Block 2 – autumn second half term

Lesson	Year 2, block 2, lesson 20
Lesson type	Practise
Lesson focus	**Strategies for learning words: selected spellings from personal lists, common errors and /dʒ/ words**
Resources needed	Spelling journals
Teaching activity	Pupils learn spellings of selected words using known strategies.

Lesson	Year 2, block 2, lesson 21
Lesson type	Teach
Lesson focus	**/s/ sound spelt 'c' before 'e', 'i' and 'y'**
Resources needed	Supporting Resource 2.10 (list of /s/ words) and 2.11 (/s/ table), blank cards
Teaching activity	Pupils generate words beginning with the /s/ sound. Write each word on a card and add some words if pupils don't suggest them (see list provided). Ask pupils to sort the words onto the table provided. What do they notice? Record their ideas. Can they think of words with /s/ in the middle or final position? How is it spelt? If the word has a /s/ followed by 'e', 'i' or 'y', then it could be spelt 'c'.

Lesson	Year 2, block 2, lesson 22
Lesson type	Practise
Lesson focus	**/s/ sound spelt 'c' before 'e', 'i' and 'y'**
Resources needed	Supporting Resource 2.12 (list of /s/ words some incorrect), spelling journals
Teaching activity	Remind pupils about what they found in the last lesson: If the word has a /s/ followed by 'e', 'i' or 'y', then it could be spelt 'c'. Stress that there is no way of telling whether it is an 's' or a 'c', we have to look at the word and see if it looks right. Give pupils the list of words with some spelt incorrectly and ask them to go through it and choose the right spellings. Check the choices that pupils have made and identify the correct spellings.

Block 2 – autumn second half term

Lesson	Year 2, block 2, lesson 23
Lesson type	Apply
Lesson focus	/s/ sound spelt 'c' before 'e', 'i' and 'y': dictation
Resources needed	Spelling journals
Teaching activity	Dictate the following sentences: *It is too soon to go out on the icy street.* *I like to cycle to school when it is sunny.* *Cinderella cycles home and eats her supper.* Write the correct sentences up on the board and get pupils to check their writing with a spelling partner. Discuss any common errors as a class.

Lesson	Year 2, block 2, lesson 24
Lesson type	Teach/Revise
Lesson focus	**Homophones (*here/hear, sun/son, one/won*)** **Revise homophones taught so far**
Resources needed	Supporting Resources 2.13 (homophones images and words) and 2.4 (homophones covered earlier)
Teaching activity	Show pupils the images and ask them what words they think they represent. You can use the images provided and those from earlier sessions. Can pupils pair them up? Show the ways in which each word is spelt and match the spelling to the image. Which spellings do pupils know? How can we remember them?

Lesson	Year 2, block 2, lesson 25
Lesson type	Practise/Apply
Lesson focus	**Homophones (*here/hear, sun/son, one/won*)** **Revise homophones taught so far**
Resources needed	Supporting Resources 2.13 (homophones images and words) and 2.4 (homophones covered earlier), spelling journals
Teaching activity	Review the ways in which each of these homophones is spelt. Point to the homophone images and ask pupils to write the correct spelling of the word.

Block 2 – autumn second half term

Lesson	Year 2, block 2, lesson 26
Lesson type	Revise
Lesson focus	/n/ **sound spelt 'kn' and 'gn' at the beginning of words** **(Include some homophones such as:** *no/know; new/knew; night/knight; not/knot*)
Resources needed	Supporting Resource 2.14 ('kn' and 'gn' word cards), spelling journals
Teaching activity	Revise the ways in which pupils can spell the /n/ sound. Most will know 'n' and 'nn'. Write or display the 'kn' and 'gn' words on the board, sound them out and read them. Draw sound buttons under them. What do pupils notice about spellings of the words? Pupils write the words in their spelling journals, talking about the spellings as they write each one and how they can be made memorable.

Lesson	Year 2, block 2, lesson 27
Lesson type	Practise
Lesson focus	/n/ **sound spelt 'kn' and 'gn' at the beginning of words**
Resources needed	Supporting Resource 2.14 ('kn' and 'gn' word cards), spelling journals
Teaching activity	Working in pairs, pupils use the sets of cards provided. They turn over the top card, read it, look carefully at how the word is spelt and then turn it back over and write it. They turn the card back over to check that they have written it correctly.

Lesson	Year 2, block 2, lesson 28
Lesson type	Teach
Lesson focus	**Strategies for learning words: saying the word in a funny way**
Resources needed	Supporting Resource 2.14 ('kn' and 'gn' word cards), spelling journals
Teaching activity	Use 'kn' and 'gn' words to practise this strategy. Pronounce the first 'k' and 'g' for example, *k-now, g-nome*. Emphasise that this strategy only works with a few spelling patterns. Pupils add these words to their spelling journals.

Block 2 – autumn second half term

Lesson	Year 2, block 2, lesson 29
Lesson type	Learn
Lesson focus	**Strategies for learning words: saying the word in a funny way**
Resources needed	Spelling journals
Teaching activity	Remind pupils of the strategy learnt in the previous lesson. Other words that might be remembered in this way are: *friend (fri-end)*, *Wednesday (Wed-nes-day), colour, said*. Take each word in turn and work out how to say it. Say it in different voices, for example, an opera singer, the smallest possible mouse, a giant etc. Now try saying the word and writing it. Check spellings and discuss errors. Pupils try this strategy by choosing a word, saying it and writing it themselves.

Lesson	Year 2, block 2, lesson 30
Lesson type	Assess
Lesson focus	**/n/ sound spelt 'kn' and 'gn' at the beginning of words: dictation**
Resources needed	Spelling journals
Teaching activity	Dictate the following sentences: *I know I have knobbly knees.* *The gnat gnawed at the meat rather than use a knife and fork.* *I got a knot in my knitting and know that I will have to start again.* Write the correct sentences up on the board and get pupils to check their writing with a spelling partner. Discuss any common errors as a class.

Year 2 Term 2 overview

Block 3 – spring first half term

	Lesson 1 Revise	Lesson 2 Teach	Lesson 3 Practise	Lesson 4 Apply	Lesson 5 Teach
Week 1	**Strategies at the point of writing: Have a go sheets**	**/aɪ/ sound spelt 'y'**	**/aɪ/ sound spelt 'y'**	**/aɪ/ sound spelt 'y'**	**Strategies for learning words: common exception words and high-frequency words** (*could, should, would*)
	Lesson 6 Teach	Lesson 7 Practise/Apply	Lesson 8 Revise	Lesson 9 Practise	Lesson 10 Teach/Practise
Week 2	**Contractions** (*can't, didn't, hasn't, it's, couldn't, I'll, they're*)	**Contractions** (*can't, didn't, hasn't, it's, couldn't, I'll, they're*)	**/l/ or /əl/ sound spelt '-le' at the end of words and following a consonant**	**/l/ or /əl/ sound spelt '-le' at the end of words and following a consonant**	**Proofreading**
	Lesson 11 Teach/Practise	Lesson 12 Teach/Practise	Lesson 13 Teach/Practise	Lesson 14 Revise/Learn	Lesson 15 Apply
Week 3	**Adding endings '-ing', '-ed', '-er', '-est' to words ending in 'e' with a consonant before it**	**Adding endings '-ing', '-ed', '-er', '-est' to words ending in 'e' with a consonant before it**	**Adding the ending 'y' to words ending in 'e' with a consonant before it**	**Strategies for learning words: selected words from this half term, focusing on polysyllabic and topic words**	**Selected words from this half term: dictation**
	Lesson 16 Teach	Lesson 17 Practise	Lesson 18 Apply	Lesson 19 Teach/Revise	Lesson 20 Practise/Apply
Week 4	**/iː/ sound spelt 'ey'**	**/iː/ sound spelt 'ey'**	**/iː/ sound spelt 'ey': dictation**	**Near homophones** (*quite/quiet*)	**Homophones and near homophones**
	Lesson 21 Teach	Lesson 22 Practise	Lesson 23 Teach/Practise	Lesson 24 Practise	Lesson 25 Assess
Week 5	**/r/ sound spelt 'wr'**	**/r/ sound spelt 'wr'**	**Common exception words** (*most, both, only*)	**Strategies for learning words: selected words from personal lists, including common exception words, topic words, /r/ words**	**/r/ sound spelt 'wr' and common exception words**
	Lesson 26 Teach	Lesson 27 Practise	Lesson 28 Apply	Lesson 29 Teach/Practise	Lesson 30 Practise/Apply
Week 6	**Adding '-ing', '-ed', '-er', '-est' and '-y' to words of one syllable ending in a single consonant after a single vowel**	**Adding '-ing', '-ed', '-er', '-est' and '-y' to words of one syllable ending in a single consonant after a single vowel**	**Adding '-ing', '-ed', '-er', '-est' and '-y' to words of one syllable ending in a single consonant after a single vowel**	**Common exception words** (*move, prove, improve, should, would, could, most, both, only*)	**Strategies at the point of writing: using a working wall**

Block 4 – spring second half term

Week 1	Lesson 1 Teach **/ɒ/ spelt 'a' after 'w' and 'qu'**	Lesson 2 Practise **Strategies for learning words: /ɒ/ spelt 'a' after 'w' and 'qu'**	Lesson 3 Assess **/ɒ/ spelt 'a' after 'w' and 'qu': dictation**	Lesson 4 Teach **Strategies for learning spellings: mnemonics**	Lesson 5 Practise **Strategies for learning spellings: mnemonics**
Week 2	Lesson 6 Revise **/ʒ/ spelt 's', segmentation and syllable clapping**	Lesson 7 Practise **/ʒ/ spelt 's'**	Lesson 8 Assess **/ʒ/ spelt 's'**	Lesson 9 Revise **Homophones (new/knew)**	Lesson 10 Teach/Practise **Homophones (there, their, they're)**
Week 3	Lesson 11 Teach **Adding '-es' to nouns and verbs ending in 'y'**	Lesson 12 Practise **Adding '-es' to nouns and verbs ending in 'y'**	Lesson 13 Apply **Adding '-es' to nouns and verbs ending in 'y'**	Lesson 14 Revise **Strategies for learning words: Look, say, cover, write, check for selected words**	Lesson 15 Practise/Apply **Strategies for learning words**
Week 4	Lesson 16 Teach **The possessive apostrophe (singular nouns)**	Lesson 17 Practise **The possessive apostrophe (singular nouns)**	Lesson 18 Apply **The possessive apostrophe (singular nouns)**	Lesson 19 Teach **Strategies at the point of writing: using an alphabetically-ordered word bank**	Lesson 20 Practise **Strategies at the point of writing: using an alphabetically-ordered word bank**
Week 5	Lesson 21 Teach **Adding suffixes '-ful' , '-less' and '-ly'**	Lesson 22 Practise **Adding suffixes '-ful' , '-less' and '-ly'**	Lesson 23 Apply **Adding suffixes '-ful' , '-less' and '-ly'**	Lesson 24 Revise/Learn: **Strategies for learning words from this half term**	Lesson 25 Assess **Words from this half term**
Week 6	Lesson 26 Revise **Contractions (can't, didn't, hasn't, it's, couldn't, I'll, they're)**	Lesson 27 Teach **Words ending '-tion'**	Lesson 28 Practise **Words ending '-tion'**	Lesson 29 Teach **Proofreading: dictionary skills**	Lesson 30 Practise **Proofreading: dictionary skills**

Block 3 – spring first half term

Lesson	Year 2, block 3, lesson 1
Lesson type	Revise
Lesson focus	**Strategies at the point of writing: Have a go sheets**
Resources needed	Have a go sheets, spelling journals
Teaching activity	Review with pupils their Have a go sheets and how well they have been using them. Discuss any aspects that the pupils raise. Remind them of the sheet inside their spelling journal (see lesson Year 2, block 1, lesson 11) that suggests things they can do if they are stuck on a spelling. During the day when pupils are writing, ensure that they are using their Have a go sheets and making choices about tricky parts of words.

Lesson	Year 2, block 3, lesson 2
Lesson type	Teach
Lesson focus	/aɪ/ **sound spelt 'y'**
Resources needed	Supporting Resource 2.15 (word cards ending 'y'), spelling journals
Teaching activity	Write the following words on the board and ask pupils to read them, segmenting them if necessary: *cry, fly, dry, try, reply, why, by* and *July*. Draw attention to the sound that appears in all of the words, where it is in the word and how it is spelt. Pupils record these words in their spelling journals.

Lesson	Year 2, block 3, lesson 3
Lesson type	Practise
Lesson focus	/aɪ/ **sound spelt 'y'**
Resources needed	Supporting Resource 2.15 (word cards ending 'y'), spelling journals, large sheets of paper on the wall
Teaching activity	Remind pupils of the focus of the session and call out several of the words from the list provided, which they segment, if necessary, and then write. Put pupils into teams of about four in front of a large piece of paper stuck on the wall, one pupil holding the pen. Call out one of the words and teams see how many times they can write the word, spelt correctly, on the sheet of paper. Each pupil writes the word once and then runs to give the pen to the next pupil, who then writes the word. How many times can they write the word in three minutes? Try several other words.

Block 3 – spring first half term

Lesson	Year 2, block 3, lesson 4
Lesson type	Apply
Lesson focus	**/aɪ/ sound spelt 'y'**
Resources needed	Supporting Resource 2.15, (word cards ending 'y'), spelling journals
Teaching activity	Pupils work in groups of three. Give each group a set of word cards. They take it in turns to pick up a card and read it out while the other two write down the word. The reader checks that the word has been spelt correctly. The next pupil then becomes the reader.

Lesson	Year 2, block 3, lesson 5
Lesson type	Teach
Lesson focus	**Strategies for learning words: common exception words and high-frequency words (could, should, would)**
Resources needed	Spelling journals, whiteboards
Teaching activity	Put *could* up on the board and read it with pupils. Add in the sound buttons and talk about the tricky part. Draw a box around the tricky parts and look at the shape closely. Ask pupils to Quickwrite the word in two minutes. Check for accuracy and discuss errors. Tell pupils that if they can spell that word, they can also spell *would* and *should*. Pupils have a go on their whiteboards. They show their spellings and discuss any errors. They have another go. Pupils practise handwriting these words.

Lesson	Year 2, block 3, lesson 6
Lesson type	Teach
Lesson focus	**Contractions (can't, didn't, hasn't, it's, couldn't, I'll, they're)**
Resources needed	Supporting Resource 2.16 (contractions dominoes), spelling journals
Teaching activity	Teach pupils what a contraction is and explore it in terms of *cannot* and *can't*. Talk about why we use contractions. Practise saying the words *contraction* and *apostrophe*. Stress that the apostrophe goes in the place of the missing letter(s). Give pairs of pupils sets of dominoes from the resource and show them how to play with them, placing them in a row, matching the corresponding words. Go through each contraction and check that pupils have matched it correctly. Pupils write the resulting chain of words in their spelling journals.

Block 3 – spring first half term

Lesson	Year 2, block 3, lesson 7
Lesson type	Practise/Apply
Lesson focus	**Contractions (*can't, didn't, hasn't, it's, couldn't, I'll, they're*)**
Resources needed	Individual whiteboards
Teaching activity	Call out the full words and ask pupils to write down contractions on their whiteboards. They hold them up to show. Discuss any errors.

Lesson	Year 2, block 3, lesson 8
Lesson type	Revise
Lesson focus	**/l/ or /əl/ sound spelt 'le' at the end of words and following a consonant.**
Resources needed	Supporting Resource 2.17 (word cards: *table, apple, bottle, little, middle*), spelling journals
Teaching activity	Focus on the target words and compare the grapheme 'le' with spellings for /l/ in other positions in words: *light, bell, help, bolt, falling, feeling*. Pupils add these words to their spelling journals and use the Highlighting tricky parts strategy to learn these words. **Note**: This is the most common spelling of this sound at the end of words.

Lesson	Year 2, block 3, lesson 9
Lesson type	Practise
Lesson focus	**/l/ or /əl/ sound spelt 'le' at the end of words and following a consonant**
Resources needed	Supporting Resource 2.17 (word cards: *table, apple, bottle, little, middle*), spelling journals
Teaching activity	Play a memory game. Use the word cards provided and display these under the visualiser or on the whiteboard. Read the words with pupils and then ask them to close their eyes while you remove one of the words. Ask pupils to write the missing word. Check their answers. Repeat with other words.

Block 3 – spring first half term

Lesson	Year 2, block 3, lesson 10
Lesson type	Teach/Practise
Lesson focus	**Proofreading**
Resources needed	Examples of pupils' writing
Teaching activity	Use an example from a pupil's writing. Model checking spellings in the first sentence. Talk about each word and why it is or isn't correct. Pupils look through the second sentence in pairs. They share what was found and discuss alternatives for errors. Pupils now look at their own writing and that of their partner. They put a line under words that they think are spelt incorrectly and have a go at correcting them.

Lesson	Year 2, block 3, lesson 11
Lesson type	Teach/Practise
Lesson focus	**Adding endings '-ing', '-ed', '-er', '-est' to words ending in 'e' with a consonant before it**
Resources needed	Spelling journals, whiteboards
Teaching activity	Write a list of verbs on the board that end in 'e' with a consonant before it: *hike, shine, hope, take, write, make, like, ride*. Show pupils that the 'e' is taken off before adding the endings '-ing', '-ed', '-er', '-est'. (Look at exceptions: *made, shone* and *took*). Show correct and incorrect versions of the words on the board. Pupils work in teams to decide which one is right and show it on a whiteboard. Pupils add these words to their spelling journals.

Lesson	Year 2, block 3, lesson 12
Lesson type	Teach/Practise
Lesson focus	**Adding endings '-ing', '-ed', '-er', '-est' to words ending in 'e' with a consonant before it**
Resources needed	Supporting Resource 2.18 ('-er' '-est' endings grid)
Teaching activity	Write on the board a list of adjectives that end in 'e' with a consonant before it: *nice, late, ripe, rude, brave*. Show pupils that the 'e' is taken off to add the endings '-er' and '-est'. Pupils practise adding the endings '-ing', '-ed', '-er', '-est' to words ending in 'e' with a consonant before it. Give pupils a copy of the grid provided to make as many words as they can by adding the suffixes.

Block 3 – spring first half term

Lesson	Year 2, block 3, lesson 13
Lesson type	Teach/Practise
Lesson focus	**Adding the ending '-y' to words ending in '-e' with a consonant before it**
Resources needed	Supporting Resource 2.19 (list of words ending in '-e')
Teaching activity	Display on the board a list of words ending in 'e' with a consonant before it: *shine, scare, stone, smoke, bone, shake.* Show pupils that the 'e' is taken off when you add'y'. Play a memory game by displaying some of the words on the list provided. Remove one word while pupils close their eyes and then ask them to write the word that has disappeared.

Lesson	Year 2, block 3, lesson 14
Lesson type	Revise/Learn
Lesson focus	**Strategies for learning words: selected words from this half term, focusing on polysyllabic and topic words**
Resources needed	Cards for selected words
Teaching activity	Prepare a selection of words learnt so far this term using mainly polysyllabic and topic words. Remind pupils of the clap and count strategy for identifying syllables. Demonstrate with a couple of words. Place pupils in groups of four to play the clap, count and draw challenge. Give each group a pile of word cards. In turn, each pupil should take the top card, read it aloud and put it face down in front of them. The rest of the group clap and count the syllables, draw a line for each syllable and write down the letters for each syllable. The card is then revealed and everyone checks their accuracy, gaining one point for the correct number of syllables and one point for each syllable spelt correctly. Repeat until each pupil has had at least one turn to read out a card and then total the points. The game can be differentiated for groups depending on the words used.

Block 3 – spring first half term

Lesson	Year 2, block 3, lesson 15
Lesson type	Apply
Lesson focus	**Selected words learnt this half term: dictation**
Resources needed	Spelling journals
Teaching activity	Dictate the following sentences using words learnt this half term: *The hiker hasn't got a kettle.* *The nicest, shiny apple was in the middle.* *I'll try not to muddle up my spellings.* *In July it's hot for the fly in the bottle.* Write the correct sentences up on the board and get pupils to check their writing with a spelling partner. Discuss any common errors as a class.

Lesson	Year 2, block 3, lesson 16
Lesson type	Teach
Lesson focus	**/iː/ sound spelt 'ey'**
Resources needed	Supporting Resource 2.20 ('ey' word list), whiteboards
Teaching activity	Read out the words on the list and ask pupils to segment them and then say the whole word. What sound can they hear in all of the words? How might it be spelt? Pupils write *key* and show it on their whiteboards. Add sound buttons and discuss the sound that the 'ey' makes. Then they try spelling some of the other words.

Lesson	Year 2, block 3, lesson 17
Lesson type	Practise
Lesson focus	**/iː/ sound spelt 'ey'**
Resources needed	Supporting Resource 2.21 ('ey' images), spelling journals
Teaching activity	Share the images. Pupils say what they are, segment the words and blend again. Remind pupils that the sound /iː/ is spelt 'ey'. Check how the pupils have spelt the words.

Block 3 – spring first half term

Lesson	Year 2, block 3, lesson 18
Lesson type	Apply
Lesson focus	/iː/ sound spelt 'ey': dictation
Resources needed	Spelling journals
Teaching activity	Dictate the following sentences: *We found the key to the donkey and monkey cage.* *It's sunny down in the valley but the sun hasn't come out up here.* Write the correct sentences up on the board and get pupils to check their writing with a spelling partner. Discuss any common errors as a class.

Lesson	Year 2, block 3, lesson 19
Lesson type	Teach/Revise
Lesson focus	**Near homophones (*quite*/*quiet*)**
Resources needed	Spelling journals
Teaching activity	Share the near homophones *quite* and *quiet* with the class and ask them to say each one, listening carefully for the differences. They put their hands up when they hear *quite* and fingers on lips when they hear *quiet*. Sound out each word and put sound buttons under each one. Which one has more phonemes? What sound does the 'e' make in *quiet*? Pupils work in pairs to create sentences using both words and then write them. Pupils add these to their spelling journals.

Lesson	Year 2, block 3, lesson 20
Lesson type	Practise/Apply
Lesson focus	**Homophones and near homophones**
Resources needed	Supporting Resource 2.22 (homophones word chart), blank 3 x 3 grid per pupil
Teaching activity	Give pupils a blank 3 x 3 grid. Put up on the board the range of homophones that have been taught so far this year (see chart provided). Pupils choose which nine words they want to write on their grid. Create sentences or definitions for each word on the chart and call them out. Pupils cross out the word if they have it on their card. For example, *This buzzes from flower to flower collecting pollen.* If they have *bee* on their cards, they can cross it out.

No Nonsense Spelling

Block 3 – spring first half term

Lesson	Year 2, block 3, lesson 21
Lesson type	Teach
Lesson focus	/r/ sound spelt 'wr'
Resources needed	Supporting Resource 2.23 (sets of cards with 'wr' and remainder of words), spelling journals
Teaching activity	Use the cards provided – one with 'wr' and the others with the remainder of the words. Put the cards together, read the word and notice the tricky parts. Pupils then record them in their spelling journals. Pairs of pupils take a set of cards and continue this activity. Read all the words with the pupils. Ensure they are clear about meaning and have written the words down correctly.

Lesson	Year 2, block 3, lesson 22
Lesson type	Practise
Lesson focus	/r/ sound spelt 'wr'
Resources needed	Supporting Resource 2.23 (sets of cards with 'wr' and remainder of words), spelling journals
Teaching activity	Model remembering how to spell the tricky parts of words. Pupils identify the tricky parts and learn how to spell the words that they need to work on. Ask each pupil to choose the trickiest word and use Quickwrite with the word. These words could be sent home for pupils to continue learning.

Lesson	Year 2, block 3, lesson 23
Lesson type	Teach/Practise
Lesson focus	Common exception words (*most, both, only*)
Resources needed	Spelling journals
Teaching activity	Write the words *most*, *both* and *only* on the board. Read the words and put the sound buttons under them. What sound does the 'o' make? Pupils practise handwriting for both words, saying them as they write them. They Quickwrite each word for two minutes. Discuss any errors and why they were made.

Block 3 – spring first half term

Lesson	Year 2, block 3, lesson 24
Lesson type	Practise
Lesson focus	**Strategies for learning words: selected words from personal lists, including common exception words, topic words and /r/ words**
Resources needed	Spelling journals
Teaching activity	Pupils identify spellings that they need to work on from their writing. They use the range of strategies to remember how to spell them, including: • Highlighting the tricky part of the word • Clapping out syllables and writing something for each syllable • Look, say, cover, write, check • Rainbow writing • Saying words in a funny way Work on two words as a whole class and then set pupils off to learn their own words.

Lesson	Year 2, block 3, lesson 25
Lesson type	Assess
Lesson focus	**/r/ sound spelt 'wr' and common exception words**
Resources needed	None
Teaching activity	Test the spelling of these words.

Lesson	Year 2, block 3, lesson 26
Lesson type	Teach
Lesson focus	**Adding '-ing', '-ed', '-er', '-est' and '-y' to words of one syllable ending in a single consonant after a single vowel**
Resources needed	Spelling journals, whiteboards
Teaching activity	Write on the board the word *pat* and show what happens when the endings are added: *pat, patted, patting*. Ask pupils what they think will happen with another example. Ask them to write the words on their whiteboards, for example, *drop, dropped, dropping*. Try another example. Show them why it would look and sound wrong if the consonant was not doubled (the vowel would be long rather than short, for example, *fater*). Pupils add these words to their spelling journals.

Block 3 – spring first half term

Lesson	Year 2, block 3, lesson 27
Lesson type	Practise
Lesson focus	**Adding '-ing', '-ed', '-er', '-est' and '-y' to words of one syllable ending in a single consonant after a single vowel**
Resources needed	Supporting Resource 2.24 (short passage and cloze exercise)
Teaching activity	Display the short passage. Ask pupils to read it and to write out all the words that they find with the double consonant and endings above.

Lesson	Year 2, block 3, lesson 28
Lesson type	Apply
Lesson focus	**Adding '-ing', '-ed', '-er', '-est' and '-y' to words of one syllable ending in a single consonant after a single vowel**
Resources needed	Supporting Resource 2.24 (short passage and cloze exercise)
Teaching activity	Revise the words and the pattern of doubling that pupils have been learning. Give pupils the same sentences as in the previous session but miss out the focus words. Read the whole text (or just one sentence) and get pupils to fill in the words as you read them.

Lesson	Year 2, block 3, lesson 29
Lesson type	Teach/Practise
Lesson focus	**Common exception words (*move, prove, improve, should, would, could, most, both, only*)**
Resources needed	Supporting Resource 2.25 (word list *move, prove* etc), whiteboards
Teaching activity	Write the words *move, prove* and *improve* on the board. Ask pupils to look closely at each word, identifying the tricky part and how they will remember it. Pupils work in small groups, each pupil with a whiteboard. Call out a word and pupils Quickwrite it for three minutes. Check that words are spelt correctly and count up how many words each team wrote. Move on to the next word and repeat until finished.

Lesson	Year 2, block 3, lesson 30
Lesson type	Practise/Apply
Lesson focus	**Strategies at the point of writing: using a working wall**
Resources needed	Working wall with common exception words, spelling journals
Teaching activity	Pupils use the working wall to find correct spellings of common exception words. They use them in their own sentences, focusing on copying them correctly.

Block 4 – spring second half term

Lesson	Year 2, block 4, lesson 1
Lesson type	Teach
Lesson focus	/ɒ/ spelt 'a' after 'w' and 'qu'
Resources needed	Spelling journals
Teaching activity	Write the following words on the board and ask pupils to sound them out and read them: *want, watch, wander, squash* and *quantity, quality, quarrel.* What do they notice about the words? Focus on the first letter(s) and the sound the 'a' makes. Pupils write the words down into their spelling journals. They identify which of the words that they can already spell and which need more work.

Lesson	Year 2, block 4, lesson 2
Lesson type	Practise
Lesson focus	**Strategies for learning words: /ɒ/ sound spelt 'a' after 'w' and 'qu'**
Resources needed	Spelling journals
Teaching activity	Write the words from the last lesson on the board again in a long line. Identify the tricky parts in each word and how they might be remembered. Pupils choose which word they want to Quickwrite and focus on how it is spelt. Cover all the words and pupils Quickwrite the word of their choice for three minutes. Uncover and check spellings. Repeat for another two or three words.

Lesson	Year 2, block 4, lesson 3
Lesson type	Assess
Lesson focus	**/ɒ/ sound spelt 'a' after 'w' and 'qu': dictation**
Resources needed	Spelling journals
Teaching activity	Dictate the following sentences and ask pupils to write them in their spelling journals. *We want to squash into the car without a quarrel to visit the beach.* *Watching us do this is always fun.* *We want to wander along the cliffs when we get to the seaside.* Write the correct sentences up on the board and get pupils to check their writing with a spelling partner. Discuss any common errors as a class.

Block 4 – spring second half term

Lesson	Year 2, block 4, lesson 4
Lesson type	Teach
Lesson focus	**Strategies for learning spellings: mnemonics**
Resources needed	Supporting Resource 2.26 (*because* image), spelling journals
Teaching activity	Explain that some words are really hard to remember but we use them a lot, for example, *because*. Write the word on the board and find the tricky parts. Tell pupils that remembering a special sentence can help them to spell the word. Write *Big elephants can always understand small elephants.* Show them the image provided. Demonstrate how it works as a mnemonic to help them to spell the word. Say the mnemonic sentence slowly and pupils write the word in their spelling journals. Have they got it right? Discuss any errors. Pupils learn the mnemonic and chant it as they write the word lots of times.

Lesson	Year 2, block 4, lesson 5
Lesson type	Practise
Lesson focus	**Strategies for learning spellings: mnemonics**
Resources needed	Spelling journals
Teaching activity	See if pupils can chant the mnemonic sentence for *because*. Chant it again and ask pupils to write the word. Is it right? Discuss any errors. Use Quickwrite for *because*. Show the word at the end. Pupils check how many times they have spelt it correctly.

Lesson	Year 2, block 4, lesson 6
Lesson type	Revise
Lesson focus	**/ʒ/ sound spelt 's', segmentation and syllable clapping**
Resources needed	Spelling journals, individual whiteboards
Teaching activity	Review clapping out the syllables in words. Ask pupils to clap out the syllables in the word *treasure*. Draw a box for each syllable. Put a line through the word to divide the syllables and look carefully at the way 'trea' is spelt. Then look at 'sure' and discuss how it sounds and is spelt. Cover up the word and ask pupils to segment the first syllable and write it in the box. Then do the same with the second syllable. Pupils check back to make sure that they have the words spelt correctly. Pupils have a go at writing *treasure* on their whiteboards. They show and discuss errors. Do the same for the word *usual*. Pupils add these words to their spelling journals.

Block 4 – spring second half term

Lesson	Year 2, block 4, lesson 7
Lesson type	Practise
Lesson focus	/ʒ/ sound spelt 's'
Resources needed	Spelling journals
Teaching activity	Pupils look carefully at the words *treasure* and *usual* and then do three minutes' Quickwrite on both words.

Lesson	Year 2, block 4, lesson 8
Lesson type	Assess
Lesson focus	/ʒ/ sound spelt 's'
Resources needed	Individual whiteboards
Teaching activity	Carry out a spelling test for the words *treasure* and *usual*. Say one of the words and pupils write it on their whiteboard and show it. Do the same for the other word.

Lesson	Year 2, block 4, lesson 9
Lesson type	Revise
Lesson focus	Homophones (*new/knew*)
Resources needed	Supporting Resources 2.27 (cards for *new* and *knew*) and 2.28 (*knew* and *new* sentences)
Teaching activity	Discuss the meanings of the words *new* and *knew* and write them on the board. You can include these optional words: *no/know; night/knight; not/knot*. Ask pupils to talk about things that they have that are *new* and what they *knew*. Give pairs of pupils cards with *new* on one and *knew* on the other. Read the first five sentences and ask pupils to hold up the correct card for the missing word. For the next five sentences pupils write the sentences out and put the correct word in.

No Nonsense Spelling

Block 4 – spring second half term

Lesson	Year 2, block 4, lesson 10
Lesson type	Teach/Practise
Lesson focus	**Homophones (*there, their, they're*)**
Resources needed	Supporting Resource 2.27 (word cards for homophones)
Teaching activity	Show pupils some sentences with *there, their* and *they're*. Discuss the different meanings of the words and the contraction *they're* for *they are*. Give pairs of pupils word cards with *there, their* and *they're* on them. Read the following sentences and ask pupils to hold up the correct card. **There** are three cakes in the tin. **They're** going to eat those cakes! **Their** cakes are delicious! **Their** house is down this road. **There** is a big dog by that gate. **They're** going swimming tonight. **Their** home learning is very hard. Are **there** any apples left? **They're** escaping out of the window! Practise other previously taught homophones as in the previous session. If different homophones have been taught, use those instead of the ones below. I ate **two** cakes. I **see** my friend every day. **One** of the cats was **blue.** I **blew** out the candles. He ran very fast and **won** the race. I went **to** the **sea.**

Lesson	Year 2, block 4, lesson 11
Lesson type	Teach
Lesson focus	**Adding '-es' to verbs and nouns ending in 'y'**
Resources needed	Supporting Resource 2.29 ('-ies' chart), individual whiteboards
Teaching activity	Show pupils the chart provided and work out together how it operates. Ask the pupils to say *he flies* and write it down. What do the pupils notice has happened to the word? How do they think *carries* might be spelt? Discuss and then pupils have a go at writing it on their whiteboards and showing their spellings. Do the same with one or two plurals. Ask pupils what they notice about the spelling of these words.

Block 4 – spring second half term

Lesson	Year 2, block 4, lesson 12
Lesson type	Practise
Lesson focus	**Adding '–es' to verbs and nouns ending in 'y'**
Resources needed	Supporting Resource 2.29 ('-ies' chart), spelling journals
Teaching activity	Use the chart from the last lesson. Pupils review what they noticed about the spelling of the words they added to the chart in the last lesson. How did they change? Ask pupils to write the phrases/clauses added to the chart in their spelling journals. Pupils compare spellings with their partners.

Lesson	Year 2, block 4, lesson 13
Lesson type	Apply
Lesson focus	**Adding '–es' to verbs and nouns ending in 'y'**
Resources needed	Supporting Resource 2.29 ('-ies' cards), spelling journals
Teaching activity	Pupils work in pairs. Give each pair of pupils pair of cards (I fly, he…). One pupil picks up a card, reads it out to their partner and then both pupils write the missing word. They do this for as many cards as they can. Check spellings as a whole class and discuss any errors.

Lesson	Year 2, block 4, lesson 14
Lesson type	Revise
Lesson focus	**Strategies for learning words: Look, say, cover, write, check for selected words**
Resources needed	Spelling journals
Teaching activity	Remind pupils of the strategy 'Look, say, cover, write, check'. Pupils choose words from the previous session not spelt correctly or any other words they want to learn. Pupils use this strategy on each word in their spelling journals.

Lesson	Year 2, block 4, lesson 15
Lesson type	Practise/Apply
Lesson focus	**Strategies for learning words**
Resources needed	Spelling journals
Teaching activity	Pupils take each of their words from the previous lesson. They look at it and then create a sentence that includes the word. They write the sentences in their spelling journals.

Block 4 – spring second half term

Lesson	Year 2, block 4, lesson 16
Lesson type	Teach
Lesson focus	**The possessive apostrophe (singular nouns)**
Resources needed	Spelling journals
Teaching activity	Ask a few pupils to give you something belonging to them, for example, a pencil, a coat, a book. Ask the group whose pencil/coat/book you have. Write up the words on the board, for example, *Megan's, Ahmed's*. Show them the apostrophe before the 's' for belonging. Practise saying the word *apostrophe* and show them how and where it is written in the words displayed. Link back to block 3, lesson 6 (see page 41) and the use of the apostrophe for contractions. Pupils add examples of words with posessive apostrophes to their spelling journals.

Lesson	Year 2, block 4, lesson 17
Lesson type	Practise
Lesson focus	**The possessive apostrophe (singular nouns)**
Resources needed	Supporting Resource 2.30 (pictures of people with belongings) *or* ask pupils to bring in a small toy and take a photograph of each pupil with their toy, spelling journals
Teaching activity	Show pictures of people holding things belonging to them. Ask pupils to generate a caption for a picture, for example *The girl's cat*. Ask pupils to choose another picture, decide on a caption together and all write it.

Lesson	Year 2, block 4, lesson 18
Lesson type	Apply
Lesson focus	**The possessive apostrophe (singular nouns)**
Resources needed	Supporting Resource 2.23 (pictures of people with belongings) *or* photographs of pupils with their own toys.
Teaching activity	Put pupils into small groups. Remind them about the possessive apostrophe and how to write it correctly. Use either the pictures provided or your own photographs of the pupils with their toys. Give each group a selection of pictures, model how to write a caption using the possessive apostrophe and ask them to write a short caption for a picture of their choice.

Block 4 – spring second half term

Lesson	Year 2, block 4, lesson 19
Lesson type	Teach
Lesson focus	**Strategies at the point of writing: using an alphabetically-ordered word bank**
Resources needed	Alphabetically-ordered word bank in the classroom
Teaching activity	This strategy is best used when pupils are writing a topic word, high-frequency word or common exception word, as these words are most likely to be in a class, table or individual word bank. The word banks could be on the classroom wall or as mats placed under books when pupils write. Model some writing from across the curriculum that requires a word from the word bank. Say that you know the word is in the word bank and you want to find it quickly. The banks are alphabetically organised, so decide whether to start at the beginning, middle or end and look for the word. Think aloud about how you are going to remember the word as you write it, for example, by chunking it, and then write it and continue writing. Make sure you model this every day for some time. Ensure that pupils are using word banks when they write.

Lesson	Year 2, block 4, lesson 20
Lesson type	Practise
Lesson focus	**Strategies at the point of writing: using an alphabetically-ordered word bank**
Resources needed	Alphabetically-ordered word bank in the classroom
Teaching activity	Ask pupils to write some silly sentences where each sentence must include a topic word, a common exception word and a high-frequency word (or other displayed words). Remind pupils to use the word banks when they need to. Check their spellings and reinforce the non-negotiables.

Block 4 – spring second half term

Lesson	Year 2, block 4, lesson 21
Lesson type	Teach
Lesson focus	**Adding suffixes '-ful', '-less' and '-ly'**
Resources needed	Supporting Resource 2.31, spelling journals
Teaching activity	Display the sentences with some of the target words in them. Talk to pupils about the meaning of '-ful', '-less' and '-ly' and how sometimes these suffixes change a verb into an adjective (*play* to *playful*) or an adjective into an adverb (*happy* to *happily*). Look carefully at the spelling of each suffix, especially: • single 'l' on '-ful' (unlike the whole word 'full'). • double 's' on '-ness' • adding 'i' before '-ly' and '-ness' where words end in 'y' with a consonant before it, for example *happily* Show how, when you add '-ly' to the '-ful' suffix, it has a double 'l', for example, *hopefully*. Pupils add them to their spelling journals.

Lesson	Year 2, block 4, lesson 22
Lesson type	Practise
Lesson focus	**Adding suffixes '-ful', '-less' and '-ly'**
Resources needed	Supporting Resource 2.32 (word matrix), spelling journals
Teaching activity	Show pupils the word matrix and model how to use this to add the suffixes. Look at which words can take which suffixes. Pupils write each word down in their spelling journals. They check that each one is a real word by discussing with their partners and trying to put the word in a sentence orally. Discuss any that pupils are unsure about as a class and double check with a dictionary. Reinforce the spelling of each suffix, especially tricky exceptions.

Lesson	Year 2, block 4, lesson 23
Lesson type	Apply
Lesson focus	**Adding suffixes '-ful', '-less' and '-ly'**
Resources needed	Spelling journals
Teaching activity	Ask pupils to use the words they created in the previous session to write some sentences. Reinforce correct punctuation. Ask pupils to check the spelling of the words with suffixes using their spelling journal or displayed words.

Block 4 – spring second half term

Lesson	Year 2, block 4, lesson 24
Lesson type	Revise/Learn
Lesson focus	**Strategies for learning words from this half term**
Resources needed	Spelling journals
Teaching activity	Pupils use known strategies to learn words from this half term, particularly common exception words – for example, mnemonics and Look, say, cover, write, check.

Lesson	Year 2, block 4, lesson 25
Lesson type	Assess
Lesson focus	**Words from this half term**
Resources needed	Spelling journals
Teaching activity	Pupils test their spelling partners on the words they have been learning in their spelling journals. Identify some examples of words that have been used in lessons to test all pupils and see which they can remember.

Lesson	Year 2, block 4, lesson 26
Lesson type	Revise
Lesson focus	**Contractions (*can't, didn't, hasn't, it's, couldn't, I'll, they're*)**
Resources needed	Supporting Resource 2.33 (cards with contractions and full versions)
Teaching activity	Display some words with contractions from the cards provided. Ask pupils what they can remember about what is special about the spelling of these words. Show the full versions and look at the changes in spelling. Remind pupils why we use contractions and practise saying the words *contraction* and *apostrophe*. Reinforce that the apostrophe goes in the place of the missing letter(s). Play a game to reinforce the spelling of contractions, for example: • Dominoes (see block 3, lesson 6) • Quickwrite Model playing Pairs. Use pairs of cards with contractions and full versions. Pupils play with a partner, putting all the cards face down on the table and taking turns to turn over two cards. If they have a matching pair, they can keep it. If not, they must turn the cards over again. The winner is the pupil with the most pairs.

Block 4 – spring second half term

Lesson	Year 2, block 4, lesson 27
Lesson type	Teach
Lesson focus	**Words ending '-tion'**
Resources needed	Spelling journals
Teaching activity	Use the following words: *station, fiction, motion, nation, section, education, foundation, competition, lotion, direction, fraction.* Ask pupils to clap and count the syllables in *station*: 'sta' / 'tion'. Ask them to spell the first part and highlight that this is a word where the /eɪ/ phoneme is spelt with single letter 'a'. Explain that the ending '–tion' is a tricky one that is not spelt as it sounds. Ask if anyone knows how it is spelt and write it on the board. Tell them there are other spellings of '–tion' but that this is the most common. Chant the letters in the word. Rub out a letter each time they chant but reinforce chanting every letter. Can they spell the word when all the letters are rubbed out? Choose another word and repeat the process. Pupils add two or three of these words to their spelling journals.

Lesson	Year 2, block 4, lesson 28
Lesson type	Practise
Lesson focus	**Words ending '-tion'**
Resources needed	Individual whiteboards
Teaching activity	Recap the previous session. Display some more of the words on the board or under a visualiser and practise reading them by clapping and counting the syllables. Then chant the letters in each word. Ask pupils to close their eyes while you remove one of the words. Pupils work with a partner to write the missing word on their whiteboards. They show the word and check the spelling. Repeat with other words.

Lesson	Year 2, block 4, lesson 29
Lesson type	Teach
Lesson focus	**Proofreading: dictionary skills**
Resources needed	Dictionary
Teaching activity	Revise the alphabet and show pupils how a dictionary works. Practise finding different letters and using the word at the top of each page (head word) to navigate. Display a commonly misspelt word. Show pupils how to use a dictionary to find the correct spelling. Teach second and third letter searching if appropriate.

Block 4 – spring second half term

Lesson	Year 2, block 4, lesson 30
Lesson type	Practise
Lesson focus	**Proofreading: dictionary skills**
Resources needed	Dictionaries, spelling journals
Teaching activity	Ask pupils to identify two or three errors in a short piece of their own work, or a piece of work displayed on the board, using the strategies previously taught. Pupils use dictionaries to look up the correct spelling and record it in their spelling journals. Ask pupils how they will learn to spell these words. Which is the tricky part? What would help pupils to learn them?

Year 2 Term 3 overview

Block 5 – summer first half term

Week 1	Lesson 1 Revise **Strategies at the point of writing: Have a go sheets**	Lesson 2 Teach **The /l/ or /əl/ sound spelt '-el' at the end of words**	Lesson 3 Practise **The /l/ or /əl/ sound spelt '-el' at the end of words**	Lesson 4 Apply **The /l/ or /əl/ sound spelt '-el' at the end of words**	Lesson 5 Revise **Proofreading: using a dictionary/ word bank**
Week 2	Lesson 6 Teach **Adding endings '-ing', '-ed', '-er', and '-est' to words ending in '-y'**	Lesson 7 Practise **Adding endings '-ing', '-ed', '-er', and '-est' to words ending in '-y'**	Lesson 8 Apply **Adding the endings '-ing', '-ed', '-er', and '-est' to words ending in '-y'**	Lesson 9 Teach/ Practise/Apply **Strategies at the point of writing: using analogy (includes dictation)**	Lesson 10 Revise/Learn **Strategies for learning words**
Week 3	Lesson 11 Teach **The /ɔː/ sound spelt 'a' before 'l' and 'll'**	Lesson 12 Practise **The /ɔː/ sound spelt 'a' before 'l' and 'll'**	Lesson 13 Teach **The /ɔː/ sound spelt 'ar' after 'w'**	Lesson 14 Practise **The /ɔː/ sound spelt 'ar 'after 'w'**	Lesson 15 Apply **Strategies for learning words: words including /ɔː/ spelt 'a' before 'l' and 'll' and /ɔː/ spelt 'ar' after 'w'**
Week 4	Lesson 16 Teach **Suffixes '-ment' and '-ness'**	Lesson 17 Practise **Suffixes '-ment' and '-ness'**	Lesson 18 Apply **Suffixes '-ment' and '-ness'**	Lesson 19 Teach **Strategies for learning words: selected words using cards**	Lesson 20 Learn **Strategies for learning words: common exception words and words from errors**
Week 5	Lesson 21 Teach **The /ɜː/ sound spelt 'or' after 'w'**	Lesson 22 Practise **The /ɜː/ sound spelt 'or' after 'w'**	Lesson 23 Assess **The /ɜː/ sound spelt 'or' after 'w': dictation**	Lesson 24 Revise **The possessive apostrophe (singular nouns)**	Lesson 25 Practise/Assess **The possessive apostrophe (singular nouns): dictation**
Week 6	Lesson 26 Teach **The /l/ or /əl/ sound spelt '-al' at the end of words**	Lesson 27 Practise **The /l/ or /əl/ sound spelt '-al' at the end of words**	Lesson 28 Apply **The /l/ or /əl/ sound spelt '-al' at the end of words**	Lesson 29 Teach **Strategies for learning words: using Look, say, cover, write and check for common exception words**	Lesson 30 Practise/Apply **Common exception words**

Block 6 – summer second half term

Week 1	Lesson 1 Revise **Spellings and concepts that pupils need to secure**	Lesson 2 Practise **Spellings and concepts that pupils need to secure**	Lesson 3 Apply **Spellings and concepts that pupils need to secure**	Lesson 4 Teach **Spellings and concepts that pupils need to secure**	Lesson 5 Practise/Apply **Spellings and concepts that pupils need to secure**
Week 2	Lesson 6 Revise **Homophones**	Lesson 7 Apply **Homophones**	Lesson 8 Teach **/ʌ/ sound spelt 'o'**	Lesson 9 Practise/Apply **/ʌ/ sound spelt 'o'**	Lesson 10 Apply **Words revised or learnt this week**
Week 3	Lesson 11 Teach **/l/ or /əl/ sounds spelt 'il' at the end of words**	Lesson 12 Practise **/l/ or /əl/ sounds spelt 'il' at the end of words**	Lesson 13 Apply **/l/ or /əl/ sounds spelt 'il' at the end of words**	Lesson 14 Revise **Strategies for learning words: common exception words**	Lesson 15 Apply **Common exception words**
The remainder of the term	Spelling lessons should now focus on the following: • Revision of all the content from the Year 2 programme • Securing spelling strategies • At the point of writing – introducing personal Have a go sheets for all writing if these have not already been introduced • After writing – developing proofreading and checking skills including using a dictionary • Learning spellings – developing children's personal spelling journals to reflect their growing independence in using taught strategies to learn new words.				

No Nonsense Spelling

Block 5 – summer first half term

Lesson	Year 2, block 5, lesson 1
Lesson type	Revise
Lesson focus	**Strategies at the point of writing: Have a go sheets**
Resources needed	Supporting Resource 2.2 (Have a go sheet)
Teaching activity	Remind pupils how to use a Have a go sheet and introduce individual sheets if pupils do not have these already. Ensure that they are available for all writing activities. Model needing to write a difficult word. What strategies could they use to have a go? • Segmenting, counting phonemes and then matching phonemes to graphemes • Chunking by syllables and then selecting graphemes • Using a GPC chart to help make the correct choice of grapheme for the tricky part of the word • Using word banks displayed in the classroom Dictate a sentence including a commonly misspelt word or word that is challenging for pupils and ask them to practise having a go using one or more of the strategies – for example, *I can see a **beautiful** big cat.* Ask: Does the word look right? Have you seen it looking like that in a book? Reinforce that pupils should continue with writing once they have tried the word once or twice.

Lesson	Year 2, block 5, lesson 2
Lesson type	Teach
Lesson focus	**The /l/ or /əl/ sound spelt '-el' at the end of words**
Resources needed	Supporting Resources 2.34 (cards with '-el' words) and 2.35 (chart with columns '-le' and '-el')
Teaching activity	Revisit the /l/ or /əl/ sounds spelt '-le' at the end of words, for example: *bottle, muddle, little*. Tell pupils that another spelling of this phoneme is '-el'. Pupils work in small groups. Give each group a set of word cards and a chart headed '-le' and '-el'. Ask them to read each word card and then put it into either the '-le' or '-el' column on the chart. Display a class version of the chart. **Note**: Keep this display for use in future weeks with other spellings for this phoneme. Pupils add two or three '-el' words to their spelling journals.

Spelling
No Nonsense

Block 5 – summer first half term

Lesson	Year 2, block 5, lesson 3
Lesson type	Practise
Lesson focus	**The /l/ or /əl/ sound spelt '-el' at the end of words**
Resources needed	Supporting Resource 2.34 (cards with '-el' words)
Teaching activity	Take pupils into the playground. Label one side of the playground with '-el' and the other with '-le'. Call out a word and pupils run to the correct side of the playground depending on the spelling of the ending. Hold up the word card and ask pupils to chant it letter by letter.

Lesson	Year 2, block 5, lesson 4
Lesson type	Apply
Lesson focus	**The /l/ or /əl/ sound spelt '-el' at the end of words**
Resources needed	Supporting Resource 2.36 ('-le' and '-el' words list), spelling journals
Teaching activity	Display a list of words with the '-le' or '-el' missed off. Ask pupils to work with their spelling partners to write the words with the correct ending. Reinforce asking 'Does it look right?' or 'Have I seen this word written like this in a book?' Check spellings as a class.

Lesson	Year 2, block 5, lesson 5
Lesson type	Revise
Lesson focus	**Proofreading: using a dictionary/word bank**
Resources needed	Dictionaries/word bank
Teaching activity	Revise using a dictionary or word bank to check and correct words you are not sure about. Ask: • Which words will we look for (for example, words from spelling journals)? • How will you remember these words? • What strategies could you use?

Block 5 – summer first half term

Lesson	Year 2, block 5, lesson 6
Lesson type	Teach
Lesson focus	**Adding endings '-ing', '-ed', '-er', '-est' to words ending in 'y'**
Resources needed	Spelling journals
Teaching activity	Use the following words: *copy, worry, happy, cry, reply, funny.* Choose one of the words from the list above and draw a chart on the board with the headings '-ing', '-ed', '-er', '-est'. Show pupils how the word is changed when adding the endings. What do they notice? (The 'y' changes to 'i 'apart from when '-ing' is added, otherwise there would be 'ii') Ask pupils to try one of the other words. (Not all the words can have all the morphemes added to them.) Try as many words as there is time for. Say the words in a sentence to check that they are real words. Pupils add the words to their spelling journals.

Lesson	Year 2, block 5, lesson 7
Lesson type	Practise
Lesson focus	**Adding endings '–ing', '-ed', '-er', '-est' to words ending in 'y'**
Resources needed	Supporting Resource 2.37 ('-ing', '-ed', '-er', '-est' matrix), spelling journals
Teaching activity	Using the matrix provided, ask pupils to make as many words as possible. After five minutes, stop them and check that they are spelling the words correctly and using the convention of 'y to 'i' apart from when adding '-ing'. Pupils continue making words.

Lesson	Year 2, block 5, lesson 8
Lesson type	Apply
Lesson focus	**Adding endings '-ing', '-ed', '-er', '-est' to words ending in 'y'**
Resources needed	Spelling journals
Teaching activity	Write one of the root words on the board and then call out the word with one of the endings. Pupils write the words down.

No Nonsense Spelling

Block 5 – summer first half term

Lesson	Year 2, block 5, lesson 9
Lesson type	Teach/Practise/Apply
Lesson focus	**Strategies at the point of writing: using analogy (includes dictation)**
Resources needed	Individual whiteboards
Teaching activity	Explain that sometimes when we don't know a word, we can use other words that are like it to help us spell. Tell them that this is called 'analogy' and explain that, for example, you may not know how to spell *right* as in 'Is this spelling right?' However you may know that on the wall you have the word *light* as part of your science display, so you can use that to help you to write *right*. Model doing this and writing *right*. Do pupils know any other words that can be made using the analogy with *light*? Put up some words on the board such as *light, ground, stick* and *late*. Ask pupils to sound them out, blend them and then put the sound buttons on them. Explain that you would like them to use one of these words to help spell *fright*. Pupils work in pairs to identify the word that will help them and then write it on their whiteboard and show. Do this for a range of words, for example, *found, brick, plate*. Tell them to highlight the part of the word that helps them. Dictate the following sentences for the pupils to write using this strategy and the displayed words to help them. *The light is bright.* *I can hear the sound.* *The cat was quick.*

Lesson	Year 2, block 5, lesson 10
Lesson type	Revise/Learn
Lesson focus	**Strategies for learning words**
Resources needed	Spelling journals
Teaching activity	Revise all the strategies pupils know for learning words. Remind pupils to use these strategies to learn words from their spelling journals and words from this week.

Block 5 – summer first half term

Lesson	Year 2, block 5, lesson 11
Lesson type	Teach
Lesson focus	**The /ɔː/ sound spelt 'a' before 'l' and 'll'**
Resources needed	Supporting Resource 2.38 (chart for spelling of /ɔː/), GPC charts, spelling journals
Teaching activity	Use the following words: *call, tall, ball, walk, talk, always* Look at GPC charts and identify common spellings for the /ɔː/ phoneme: 'or', 'a', 'au', 'aw', 'oor'. See if pupils can think of some words for each of these spellings and write them up in the chart to display. If they think of other more unusual spellings of the phoneme, record these in another column. Focus on the ones spelt with just 'a'. What do they notice? Tell them the rule that the /ɔː/ sound is usually spelt as 'a' before 'l' or 'll'. Tell pupils to look at the tricky ones where they can't hear the 'l'. What can they do to help them remember these? Pupils add the words to their spelling journals.

Lesson	Year 2, block 5, lesson 12
Lesson type	Practise
Lesson focus	**The /ɔː/ sound spelt 'a' before 'l' and 'll'**
Resources needed	Supporting Resource 2.39 (passage with /ɔː/), spelling journals
Teaching activity	Ask pupils to read the short passage and find all the words with /ɔː/ spelt 'a' before 'l' and 'll'. They write each word that they find correctly.

Lesson	Year 2, block 5, lesson 13
Lesson type	Teach
Lesson focus	**The /ɔː/ sound spelt 'ar' after 'w'**
Resources needed	Class chart from Lesson 11, spelling journals
Teaching activity	Use the following words: *war, warm, towards, ward, warn.* Revisit the spellings for the sound /ɔː/ and tell pupils that there is another spelling of this sound that is unusual and occurs after 'w'. Show them the words above and ask them to identify the spelling of /ɔː/ in these words. Look to see if any of these words were generated earlier in the week and add any new ones to the class chart. Pupils add two or three words to their spelling journals and practise handwriting this pattern, focusing on joining 'w' at the top, 'a' at the bottom and 'r' at the top.

Block 5 – summer first half term

Lesson	Year 2, block 5, lesson 14
Lesson type	Practise
Lesson focus	**The /ɔː/ sound spelt 'ar' after 'w'**
Resources needed	Coloured pencils, spelling journals
Teaching activity	Use Rainbow writing. Ask pupils to write one of the words from the previous session in large, clear, joined handwriting. Then ask them to use a coloured pencil to trace over the word. They trace it three times using a different colour each time. Repeat with other words.

Lesson	Year 2, block 5, lesson 15
Lesson type	Apply
Lesson focus	**Strategies for learning words: words including /ɔː/ spelt 'a' before 'l' and 'll' and /ɔː/ spelt 'ar' after 'w'**
Resources needed	Spelling journals
Teaching activity	Apply previously taught strategies to current word lists including the /ɔː/ sound spelt 'a' before 'l' and 'll' and the /ɔː/ sound spelt 'ar' after 'w' – for example, • Look, say, cover, write, check • Rainbow writing • Highlighting or boxing the tricky bit and taking a 'photograph' of it • Writing it in the air/on your hand/on a partner's back,

Lesson	Year 2, block 5, lesson 16
Lesson type	Teach
Lesson focus	**Suffixes '-ment' and '-ness'**
Resources needed	Supporting Resource 2.40 ('-ment', '-ness' matrices)
Teaching activity	Share the two matrices with the class and together create words from them. What do they notice about adding '-ness' to words that end in 'y'? Remind pupils about what happened when they added other suffixes to words ending in 'y', for example, *copy, copier; happy, happily, happier, happiest*. Share the words that pupils have made. Discuss what the words mean. The suffix '-ness' changes an adjective to a noun and means 'the state of being', for example, the state of being happy or sad.

Block 5 – summer first half term

Lesson	Year 2, block 5, lesson 17
Lesson type	Practise
Lesson focus	**Suffixes '–ment' and '-ness'**
Resources needed	Supporting Resource 2.40 ('-ment', '-ness' matrices)
Teaching activity	In groups of three, pupils take it in turns to create a word from the matrices. They read it out to the others, who then try to spell it. Get them to check their spellings and, if wrong, look closely and then write the word three times.

Lesson	Year 2, block 5, lesson 18
Lesson type	Apply
Lesson focus	**Suffixes '–ment' and '–ness'**
Resources needed	Supporting Resource 2.40 ('-ment', '-ness' matrices), spelling journals
Teaching activity	Show pupils a range of the root words that they have been learning this week. Ask them to write the root word plus the suffix in their spelling journals.

Lesson	Year 2, block 5, lesson 19
Lesson type	Teach
Lesson focus	**Strategies for learning words: selected words using cards**
Resources needed	Cards for writing selected words on, spelling journals
Teaching activity	Pupils have already been introduced to the strategy of finding the tricky part of a word and trying to remember how to spell that part. Choose common exception words and words not spelt correctly in pupils' work to learn. Write these on cards. Show a word and model finding the tricky part and ways that you might remember it. Then model writing the word again and checking it. Pupils work on their own spellings, writing them on cards. The words on cards could go home for further learning.

Lesson	Year 2, block 5, lesson 20
Lesson type	Learn
Lesson focus	**Strategies for learning words: common exception words and words from errors**
Resources needed	Pupils' word cards from the previous lesson, spelling journals
Teaching activity	Pupils work in pairs. They take it in turns to choose one of the cards for their partners, read it out and ask their partners to write it in their spelling journals. They then check it.

Block 5 – summer first half term

Lesson	Year 2, block 5, lesson 21
Lesson type	Teach
Lesson focus	**The /ɜː/ sound spelt 'or' after 'w'**
Resources needed	Supporting Resource 2.41 (image cards), individual whiteboards
Teaching activity	Use the following words: *word, work, worm, world, worth, worse, worst.* Show pupils the images and ask them to work out what words they stand for. For each word ask pupils to sound it out and, as they do so, write the word underneath. Pupils write the word on their whiteboards and add the sound buttons. What do they notice about the words?

Lesson	Year 2, block 5, lesson 22
Lesson type	Practise
Lesson focus	**The /ɜː/ sound spelt 'or' after 'w'**
Resources needed	Supporting Resource 2.41 (word and image cards), spelling journals
Teaching activity	Pupils work in small groups. Give each group cards with the images and words on. They choose one card, turn it face down and the whole group writes it. They then turn the card over and check that they have spelt the word correctly. If not, they rewrite the word three times after looking at the tricky part again. They repeat with another image.

Lesson	Year 2, block 5, lesson 23
Lesson type	Assess
Lesson focus	**The /ɜː/ sound spelt 'or' after 'w': dictation**
Resources needed	Spelling journals
Teaching activity	Dictate the following sentences: *It will not be worth watching a worm as it works down into the soil.* *The world is full of worms that are on the path and grass.* Write the correct sentences up on the board and get pupils to check their writing with a spelling partner. Discuss any common errors as a class.

Spelling
No Nonsense

Block 5 – summer first half term

Lesson	Year 2, block 5, lesson 24
Lesson type	Revise
Lesson focus	**The possessive apostrophe (singular nouns)**
Resources needed	Supporting Resource 2.42 (apostrophe sentences), spelling journals
Teaching activity	Display some words with the possessive apostrophe on the board. Ask pupils what they notice about these words. Can they remember what this is called and why it is used? Look at a sentence from the supporting resource with an apostrophe missing. Ask pupils to spot where it should go. Display another sentence and ask pupils to copy it, putting in the apostrophe correctly.

Lesson	Year 2, block 5, lesson 25
Lesson type	Practise/Assess
Lesson focus	**The possessive apostrophe (singular nouns): dictation**
Resources needed	Spelling journals
Teaching activity	Dictate sentences using the possessive apostrophe. Check that pupils have applied it correctly. *That is Anna's coat.* *Please give me Hamid's ball.* *This car's lights are very dirty.* *Where is the girl's book?*

Lesson	Year 2, block 5, lesson 26
Lesson type	Teach
Lesson focus	**The /l/ or /əl/ sound spelt '-al' at the end of words** (*metal, pedal, capital, hospital, animal, petal*; and with suffix '-al', *medical, magical*)
Resources needed	Supporting Resource 2.43 (cards with '-al' words), spelling journals
Teaching activity	Remind pupils about the spellings that they have already learnt for the /l/ or /əl/ sound ('-le' and '-el'). Display the words that they collected in block 5, lesson 2 (see page 63). Tell pupils that they are going to learn another spelling of this phoneme. Ask them to write the words *animal, petal* and *metal* and compare with their partner. What have they written for the final phoneme? Display the correct spelling of the words and other words with this pattern (see cards provided). Ask pupils to practise writing one of the words on their partner's back with their finger. Can their partner work out which word they have written? Pupils add some of the words to their spelling journals.

Block 5 – summer first half term

Lesson	Year 2, block 5, lesson 27
Lesson type	Practise
Lesson focus	**The /l/ or /əl/ sound spelt '-al' at the end of words**
Resources needed	Supporting Resources 2.43 (cards with '-al' words), spelling journals
Teaching activity	Practise handwriting using the '-al' words from the previous lesson. Practise joining the 'a' at the bottom and making sure that the 'l' is the correct height.

Lesson	Year 2, block 5, lesson 28
Lesson type	Apply
Lesson focus	**The /l/ or /əl/ sound spelt '-al' at the end of words**
Resources needed	Supporting Resources 2.44 (cards with '-le', '-el', '-al'), individual whiteboards
Teaching activity	Give pairs of pupils three cards with '-le', '-el' and '-al' on them. Read out some words from previous sessions with the three different spellings of the /l/ or /əl/ phoneme taught so far. Ask pupils to have a go at writing the word on their whiteboards. Hold up the correct grapheme card for that word. Show them the correct spelling and chant the letters together.

Lesson	Year 2, block 5, lesson 29
Lesson type	Teach
Lesson focus	**Strategies for learning words: using Look, say, cover, write, check for common exception words**
Resources needed	Common exception words for Year 2 (page 79)
Teaching activity	Most of these words should have already been covered in previous sessions so now is the time to ensure that pupils can spell these words correctly. Show pupils the list of words and ask them to choose some that they would like to be able to spell correctly. Model for pupils how to use Look, say, cover, write and check. Pupils try it out for themselves on a couple of their words.

Block 5 – summer first half term

Lesson	Year 2, block 5, lesson 30
Lesson type	Practise/Apply
Lesson focus	**Common exception words**
Resources needed	Common exception words for Year 2 (page 79)
Teaching activity	Choose some of the words that pupils have worked on in the previous session. Call out one of the words and pupils write that word on their whiteboards. Show spellings and discuss errors. Do this for five or six of the commonly chosen words. Pupils who have spelt some of these words incorrectly use Quickwrite on them, working hard to remember the part they got wrong.

Block 6 – summer second half term

Lesson	Year 2, block 6, lessons 1–5
Lesson type	Revise
Lesson focus	**Spellings and concepts that pupils need to secure**
Resources needed	Spelling journals
Teaching activity	These five lessons provide an opportunity to revise key concepts, words and spelling patterns that have been taught in preparation for end of year assessments, for example, Year 2 SATs. Pupils need to practise spelling words in a similar context to the end of year assessment.

Spelling
No Nonsense

Block 6 – summer second half term

Lesson	Year 2, block 6, lesson 6
Lesson type	Revise
Lesson focus	**Homophones**
Resources needed	Supporting Resource 2.45 (homohone word cards)
Teaching activity	Stick enlarged versions of word cards with any of the known homophones around the hall or outside area. Read one of the sentences below containing a homophone and ask pupils to run to the correct place. Say the sentence together and chant the letters in the word. *There are [give number] children in our class.* *They're the best children in the school!* *Their teacher is great.* *I like to play spelling games.* *Have you got two cakes?* *I like cakes too.* *The sea is very choppy today.* *I can see huge waves.* *Can you hear that dog barking?* *I'll put your coat here.* *It's quite warm today.* *What a quiet classroom!* *I saw a great big bear.* *The trees are bare in the winter.* *The sun shone brightly.* *My son is six.* *He won the gold cup.* *We have one cat.* *I want to be an explorer.* *That bee is buzzing loudly!* *The wind blew strongly.* *Where is my blue hat?* *At night, I go to bed.* *The knight rode to the castle.*

Block 6 – summer second half term

Lesson	Year 2, block 6, lesson 7
Lesson type	Apply
Lesson focus	**Homophones**
Resources needed	Homophone sentences from previous lesson, spelling journals
Teaching activity	Read the same sentences that pupils practised in the previous lesson. Ask them to write down either the whole sentence or just the homophones. Check their answers and reinforce the correct spellings.

Lesson	Year 2, block 6, lesson 8
Lesson type	Teach
Lesson focus	**/ʌ/ sound spelt 'o'**
Resources needed	Supporting Resource 2.46 (word list: *other, mother, brother, nothing, none, Monday*), spelling journals, individual whiteboards
Teaching activity	Put the words from the list up on the board and ask pupils to read them in pairs. Add sound buttons once they have read them. What do they notice about the words? Cover up the words, say one word and ask pupils to sound it out and then write it. They underline the tricky part of the word and show on their whiteboards. Have they got the 'o'? Discuss any errors and why they might have happened. Pupils write the word again. Do this for as many of the words as you have time for. Pupils add the words to their spelling journals.

Lesson	Year 2, block 6, lesson 9
Lesson type	Practise/Apply
Lesson focus	**/ʌ/ sound spelt 'o'**
Resources needed	Spelling journals, Supporting Resource 2.47 (passage with errors)
Teaching activity	Ask pupils to read the passage with spelling errors for the focus GPC. How many errors can they spot? Ask them to rewrite the passage with the correct spellings.

Lesson	Year 2, block 6, lesson 10
Lesson type	Apply
Lesson focus	**Words revised or learnt this week**
Resources needed	Spelling journals
Teaching activity	In pairs, ask pupils to write silly sentences using any of the words revised or learnt this week.

Block 6 – summer second half term

Lesson	Year 2, block 6, lesson 11
Lesson type	Teach
Lesson focus	/l/ or /əl/ sounds spelt 'il' at the end of words
Resources needed	Supporting resource 2.34 (previously used in block 5, lessons 2-3)
Teaching activity	Remind pupils of the /l/ and /əl/ sounds at the end of words and the graphemes they have learnt so far to represent them. Show them the chart with the words they collected before. Which is the most common spelling of this sound? Show pupils the following words: *pencil, fossil, nostril, stencil.* How is the phoneme spelt in these words? Tell pupils that this is a very unusual spelling. Add them to the display of the different spellings in a new column. Pupils add the words to their spelling journals and practise handwriting them.

Lesson	Year 2, block 6, lesson 12
Lesson type	Practise
Lesson focus	/l/ or /əl/ sounds spelt 'il' at the end of words
Resources needed	Supporting Resource 2.48 (wordsearch), spelling journals
Teaching activity	Ask pupils to find as many /l/ or /əl/ words spelt in the four different ways as they can in the wordsearch. They should write each word down as they circle it. Tell them that there are 16 words to find. (**Answers**: *muddle, fossil, metal, parcel, animal, pencil, hospital, apple, angel, label, purple, circle, puddle, petal, bubble, table*)

Lesson	Year 2, block 6, lesson 13
Lesson type	Apply
Lesson focus	/l/ or /əl/ sounds spelt 'il' at the end of words
Resources needed	Whiteboards
Teaching activity	Play a memory game with the /l/ or /əl/ words. See block 3, lesson 9 for an explanation of the game. Display a range of words from the previous session with the different endings. Ask pupils to look at them carefully and chant some of the trickier ones. Tell pupils to close their eyes and try to remember them. Remove or cover one of the words and ask pupils to write the missing word on their whiteboards. Reveal the word and check spellings.

Block 6 – summer second half term

Lesson	Year 2, block 6, lesson 14
Lesson type	Revise
Lesson focus	**Strategies for learning words: common exception words**
Resources needed	Spelling journals
Teaching activity	Ask pupils to tell you all the different ways that they now know to learn their spellings. Make a list to display all of the strategies that they know. Display some of the common exception words that pupils are finding difficult. Which strategy do they think would help them to learn each word? Pupils record the words in their spelling journals and start using the strategies to learn the words – for example: • Look, say, cover, write, check • Tracing over and Rainbow writing • Highlighting the tricky bit • Making up a mnemonic • Saying the word in a funny way

Lesson	Year 2, block 6, lesson 15
Lesson type	Apply
Lesson focus	**Common exception words**
Resources needed	Spelling journals
Teaching activity	Pupils use the strategies discussed in the previous session. Assess pupils by asking them to write three of the words in a silly sentence.

Common exception words for Year 2

door	even	sugar
floor	great	eye
poor	break	could
because	steak	should
find	pretty	would
kind	beautiful	who
mind	after	whole
behind	fast	any
child	last	many
children	past	clothes
wild	father	busy
climb	class	people
most	grass	water
only	pass	again
both	plant	half
old	path	money
cold	bath	Mr
gold	hour	Mrs
hold	move	parents
told	prove	Christmas
every	improve	
everybody	sure	

(and/or others according to programme used)

Year 2 Supporting Resources

Error Analysis template   2.1

Name _____   Class _____   Date _____

Common exception words	GPC (includes rare GPCs and vowel digraphs)	Homophones	Prefixes and suffixes	Word endings	Other

No Nonsense Spelling

Have a go template   2.2

My column	Teacher's column	My column	Teacher's column

GPC chart 2.3

These charts show the phonemes of English represented by the International Phonetic Alphabet together with their common grapheme representations. All Phase 5 GPCs are included together with other less common grapheme choices needed in Year 2 and above. The correspondences in the table are based on Received Pronunciation and could be significantly different in other accents. One example word is provided for each phoneme to support teachers unfamiliar with IPA. Other examples can be found in Appendix 1 of the National Currciulum.

Consonant GPCs

/b/ bat	/d/ dog	/ð/ mother	/dʒ/ jug	/f/ fish	/g/ goat	/h/ hand	/j/ yawn	/k/ cat	/l/ and /əl/ lamp, bottle	/m/ mouse	/n/ nail
b bb	d dd	th	j g ge dge	f ff ph	g gg	h	y	c k ck ch q	l ll le el al il	m mm mb	n nn kn gn pn mn

/ŋ/ wing	/θ/ thumb	/p/ pin	/r/ rain	/s/ sun	/ʃ/ ship	/t/ tap	/tʃ/ chick	/v/ van	/w/ watch	/z/ zip
ng n(k)	th	p	r rr wr	s ss se c ce	sh ch ti ci ss(ion, ure) s (ion, ure	t tt	ch tch t	v ve	w wh u	z zz ze s se x

Note: The letter **x** in English frequently represents 2 adjacent consonant phonemes /k/ and /s/, for example in the word **box**.

Vowel GPCs

/ɑː/ arm	/ɒ/ hot	/æ/ cat	/aɪ/ pie	/aʊ/ cow	/ɛ/ hen	/eɪ/ day	/ɛə/ pair	/əʊ/ boat	/ɪ/ pin
ar a	o a	a	igh i-e ie i y	ow ou	e ea	ai ay a-e a ei eigh ey	air are ear	ow oa oe o-e o	i y e

/ɪə/ cheer	/iː/ bean	/ɔː/ fork	/ɔɪ/ boy	/ʊ/ book	/ʊə/ cure	/uː/ blue	/ʌ/ cup	/ɜː/ girl
ear eer ere	ea ee e-e ie y ey e ei eo	or oor ore aw au our a al ar	oy oi	oo u oul	ure our	oo u-e ue ew ui ou ough	u o	er ir ur or ear

Note: The symbol /ə/, known as "schwa" represents the unstressed phoneme in many English words. It can be spelt in many different ways, for example **er** as in farm**er**.

sea	see
blue	blew
flour	flower
bear	bare
bee	be
whole	hole

Year 2 – Block 1 – Lesson 27 2.5

m	i	n	d	l	n	s	f
k	c	k	f	k	f	b	i
d	h	i	i	n	d	n	n
l	i	n	n	n	s	b	d
i	l	d	i	l	r	m	e
h	f	h	k	i	m	i	b
c	e	l	m	w	i	l	d
b	w	d	i	l	d	c	k

Year 2 – Block 2 – Lesson 8 2.6

to	two	too

Year 2 – Block 2 – Lessons 16, 19   2.7

j	ge	dge	g

j	ge	dge	g
jacket jar jog join jig	village change huge age	badge edge dodge fudge bridge	giant giraffe gentleman gem gerbil

Year 2 – Block 2 – Lesson 17   2.8

Year 2 – Block 2 – Lesson 19   2.9

jacket	village	badge	giant
jar	change	edge	giraffe
jog	huge	dodge	gentleman
join	age	fudge	large
fridge	gentle		

Year 2 – Block 2 – Lesson 21   2.10

city	race	ice	city	fancy
site	soon	supper	sat	settle
Cinderella	cycle	celery	circle	cat
cone	custard			

Year 2 – Block 2 – Lesson 21   2.11

sa	**ca**
se	**ce**
si	**ci**
so	**co**
su	**cu**

Year 2 – Block 2 – Lesson 22   2.12

face	fase	ise	ice
sity	city	pencil	pensil
once	onse	icy	isy
sycle	cycle	circle	sircle

Year 2 – Block 2 – Lessons 24-25   2.13

one	won
hear	here
sun	son

Year 2 – Block 2 – Lessons 26–28 2.14

knot	know	knee	gnat	gnaw
knife	knit	kneecap	knobbly	gnome
knight	knew			

Year 2 – Block 3 – Lessons 2–4 2.15

cry	dry	July	fly
try	reply	why	by

Year 2 – Block 3 – Lesson 6 2.16

cannot	hasn't

has not	it's

it is	couldn't

could not	didn't

did not	I'll

I will	can't

Year 2 – Block 3 – Lessons 8 and 9   2.17

apple	muddle	bottle	little	middle
marble	table	kettle	bobble	people

Year 2 – Block 3 – Lesson 12   2.18

nice late ripe rude brave hike ride write	er
	est

Year 2 – Block 3 – Lesson 13   2.19

shine	scare	smoke
bone	stone	shake

Year 2 – Block 3 – Lesson 16   2.20

donkey	key	monkey	valley
chimney	honey	money	alley

Year 2 – Block 3 – Lesson 17 — 2.21

Year 2 – Block 3 – Lesson 20 — 2.22

quite	quiet	be	bee
hear	here	won	one
see	sea	flour	flower
new	knew	bear	bare
son	sun	blue	blew

Year 2 – Block 3 – Lessons 21 and 22 — 2.23

wr	ap	iggle	estler	ist
ite	itten	ote	ong	eck

Year 2 – Block 3 – Lessons 27 and 28   2.24

The fattest bear hummed the saddest tune he knew as he was running up the hill. He clapped his hands, patted his head and then suddenly slipped and dropped his pot of runny honey.

The _____ bear _____ the _____tune he knew as he was _____ up the hill. He_____ his hands, _____his head and then suddenly _____ and _____ his pot of _____ honey.

Year 2 – Block 3 – Lesson 29   2.25

move	prove	improve
should	would	could
most	both	only

Year 2 – Block 4 – Lesson 4   2.26

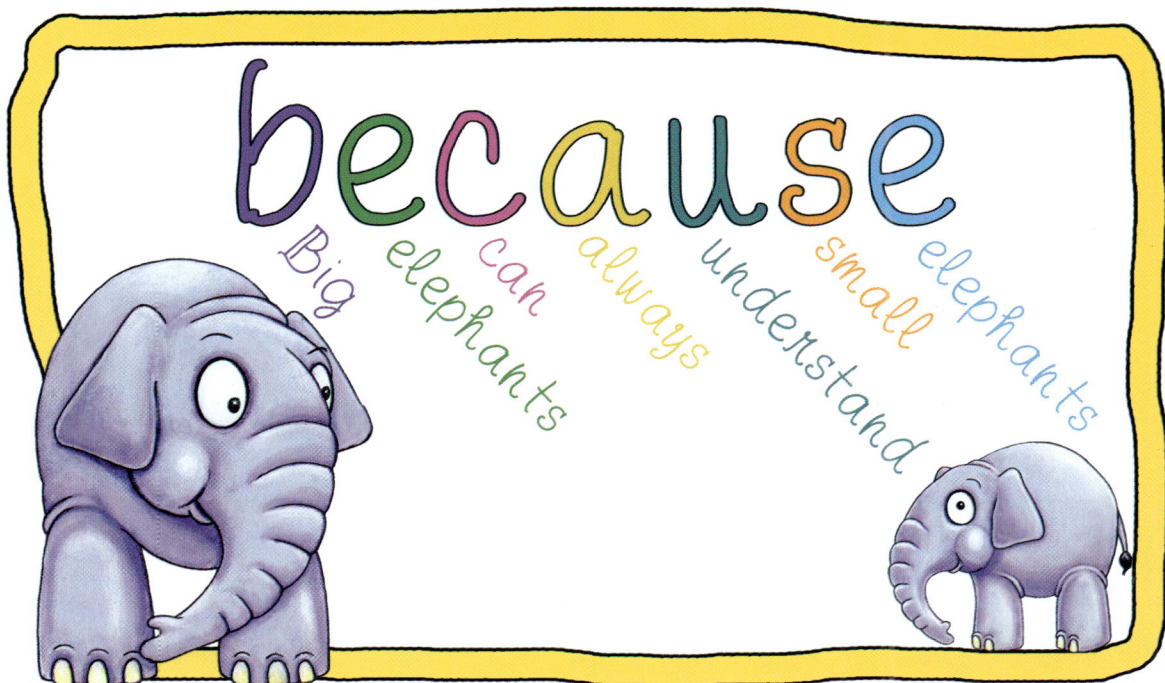

because

Big elephants can always understand small elephants

Year – Block 4 – Lessons 9 and 10 | 2.27

one	won	sea	see
blue	blew	two	to
new	knew	no	know
not	knot	night	knight
there	their	they're	knew
new			

Year 2 – Block 4 – Lesson 9 | 2.28

I have a new pair of shorts.
She knew the right answer.
She moved into her new house.
I knew his house had a red door.
The class knew that 2 + 2 = 4.
My teacher is _____to the school.
Are your shoes _____?
He _____that was the way to go.
We _____that you would come back.
The baby is a _____born.

Year 2 – Block 4 – Lessons 11 and 13 | 2.29

I fly	he	I carry	he
I cry	he	I reply	he
I copy	he	one baby	two
one lady	two	one party	two
one jelly	two	one lorry	two

Year 2 – Block 4 – Lessons 17 and 18   2.30

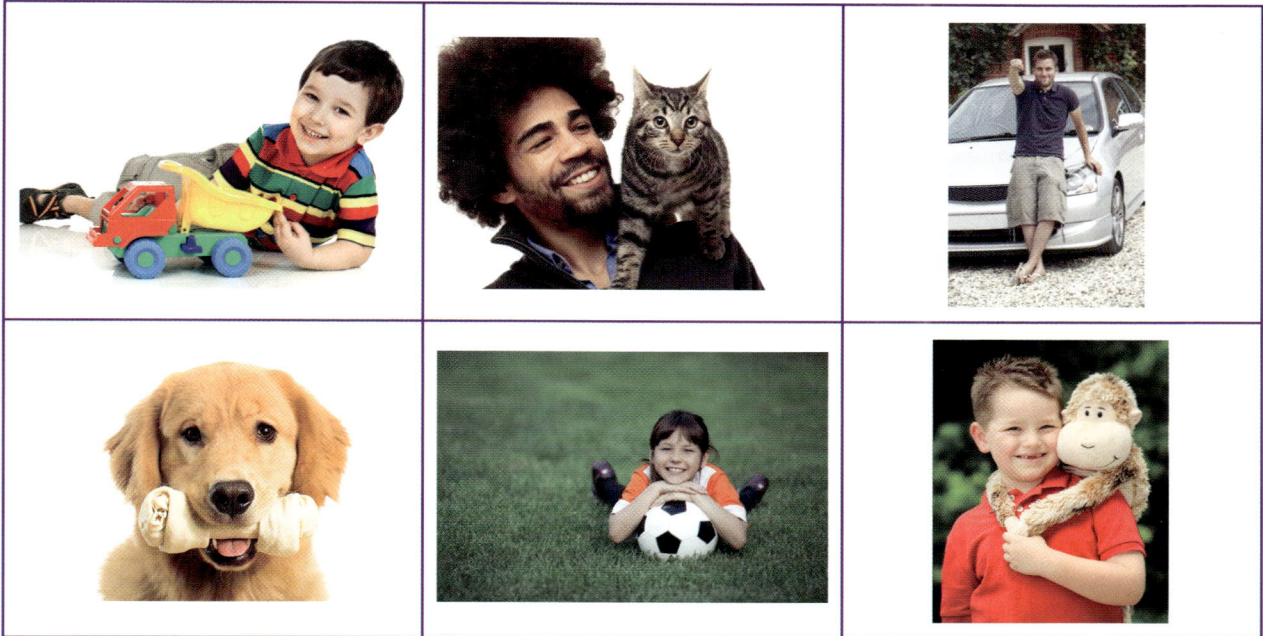

Year 2 – Block 4 – Lesson 21   2.31

Be **careful** when you are carrying eggs!
The **playful** kitten batted the toy mouse.
I am **hopeful** that tomorrow it will be sunny for our trip.
It was **hopeless**! The rain poured down all day.
The trip started **badly** as the **careless** teacher lost all the packed lunches.
The children shouted **happily** when the teacher bought them all an ice cream.

Year 2 – Block 4 – Lesson 22   2.32

bad play hope care happy sad colour harm	-ful -less	-ly

Year 2 – Block 4 – Lesson 26 2.33

can't	doesn't	I'll	they're	he's
cannot	does not	I will	they are	he is
won't	it's	I'm	wasn't	couldn't
will not	it is	I am	was not	could not

Year 2 – Block 5 – Lessons 2 and 3 2.34

middle	tickle	apple	little
circle	table	giggle	puddle
camel	tunnel	towel	tinsel
parcel	angel	squirrel	label

Year 2 – Block 5 – Lesson 2 2.35

-le	-el

Spelling
No Nonsense

Year 2 – Block 5 – Lesson 4   2.36

midd cam bott padd tunn app squirr ang	-le -el

Year 2 – Block 5 – Lesson 7   2.37

copy worry happy cry reply funny	er est ed ing

Year 2 – Block 5 – Lesson 11   2.38

or	a	au	aw	oor

There was once a very tall man called Mr Chalk who lived with his dog, cat and also a cheeky hamster. Every day, he put on his hat and coat in the hallway, picked up a ball and called, 'Come on, Fido! It's time for your walk.'

Fido and his owner always went the same way so that Mr Chalk could have a talk with his friend Bob at his flower stall in the market. One day, as they passed the old castle walls, they noticed a strange shape stalking along through the grass. Just then, the rain started to fall in enormous splashy drops so they forgot the odd shape and ran to the market hall as fast as they could.

fair sad kind tidy lovely silly nasty happy willing fit foolish	ness	enjoy employ docu oint state move	ment

Year 2 – Block 5 – Lessons 21 and 22   2.41

word	work
worm	world
worth	

The cats basket was in the corner.

I went to Lolas house yesterday.

My mums car is bright red.

metal	pedal	animal	petal
hospital	capital	medical	magical

le	el	al

there	they're	their
to	two	too
sea	see	here
quite	quiet	hear
bear	bare	one
sun	son	won
be	bee	blue
night	knight	blew

Year 2 – Block 6 – Lesson 8   2.46

other	brother
mother	nothing
Monday	none

Year 2 – Block 6 – Lesson 12   2.47

On Munday I went to visit my muther and my bruther. There was nothing to eat in the house so I set off to see if my uther bruther had sum cakes.

s	a	n	i	f	o	s	s	i	l
m	i	d	d	p	e	l	a	l	m
u	d	d	l	e	m	e	t	a	l
d	p	u	r	p	l	e	s	c	g
d	n	c	b	e	t	e	f	i	h
l	j	a	b	k	l	b	o	r	p
e	l	a	p	b	r	s	l	c	t
a	l	b	b	e	c	f	w	l	a
d	n	u	f	a	n	e	l	e	n
t	b	l	e	i	l	c	u	v	i
p	a	r	c	e	l	e	i	n	m
x	t	l	f	a	l	g	n	l	a
b	p	a	l	e	s	o	w	d	l
h	e	t	p	u	d	d	l	e	l
l	t	i	c	v	b	n	e	m	s
e	a	p	a	e	l	l	d	m	p
g	l	s	g	r	p	a	y	j	k
n	d	o	r	p	b	m	a	t	m
a	k	h	a	l	t	a	b	l	e

Notes

Notes

Notes

Notes

Notes